The infinite faces of God

A manual explaining how to discover the nature of God
and oneself as inseparable and overcome all fears

The infinite faces of God

A manual explaining how to discover the nature of God
and oneself as inseparable and overcome all fears

Max Corradi

Jaborandi Publishing

Other books by the author:

The seven Laws of Reality and Being
A manual about the Seven Hermetic Principles which govern reality and phenomena Jaborandi Publishing

Low dose medicine
Healing without side effects using low dose cytokines, interleukins, hormones, and neurotrophines
Jaborandi Publishing

Cures without side effects
Practical healing manual of the most essential and effective biotherapy treatments
Jaborandi Publishing

No Age Ontology
The Joy of Timelessness
Jaborandi Publishing

Contents

Chapter 4 - How to discover the Principle of Pure Being and how to apply this knowledge in one's perception of reality

I dedicate this book to my spiritual Teachers and to the joy and fulfilment of all beings.

May all beings realize their true nature and may all their positive wishes be fulfilled and become a source of joy.

May the illusion of poverty, illness, fear and death dissolve into the timeless Awareness of Pure Being.

'Know thyself, and thou shalt know the Universe and God'.

Pythagoras

Introduction

In each and every sentient being no matter how small or strange you must be able to see God indivisible from yourself.

This book is the second of a series of books describing Reality and Being as a self perception of a timeless Mind called God which rests at the root of our experience and is beyond all opposites and identities.

In this book I've tried to summarize in a very essential way how all the main theistic religions and the ancient hermetic traditions point to the same non-conceptual Truth regarding Reality and Being, and in particular, how the field of phenomenal reality as self perception is governed by unchanging Laws or Principles which can be known and utilized in order to achieve a more joyful and fulfilled experience of life and overcome all fears.

The aim is to give the reader a 'map' or a clue to some of the questions that underlie our basic human experience about the nature of reality and it is based on many years of studies and practice and also my own personal experience.

While reading this and my previous book, one should not remain attached to the 'finger pointing at the moon', but one should try to look at the moon directly, or rather, one should try to experience 'the moon' directly as a personal experience.

Moreover, one should never regard the word God as meaning something or someone outside of oneself but simply as one's own already complete and accomplished nature of Pure Being equivalent to the totality of all fields of experience.

'And ye shall know the truth, and the truth shall make you free'.

John 8:32

Chapter 1

The Principle of God

'I am God declaring the end from the beginning, and from ancient times, things that are not yet done'.

Isaiah 46:9, 10

God is a condition of Being not an individual being with an identity and a personality, God is a pure and infinite field of energy potentiality, a timeless empty Awareness beyond the limitation of one and many, playing with itself through an infinite number of beings which are none other than itself.

In a nutshell God is you, but not the ego-personality which you regard as 'you' or 'me' or others, but you as the all pervading Awareness of Pure Being – all creating Mind, beyond one and many, which is the nature – potentiality at the base or core of what you think you are. Christ meant exactly that when he said: *'I and my Father are one' (John 10:30).*

God is an idea that man has tried to objectify in various forms, although it always remains formless pure Awareness. It is the universal substance, beyond male and female, the life that animates the substance, and the love that binds it together.

The mistake that mankind has been making all along has always been to consider God the 'Creator' of heaven and earth as a separate individual being, **when in fact the Creator is simply the all pervading potentiality of Being which is the nature of oneself – an all creating Awareness of Pure Being beyond identities and the limitations of one and many, good and bad which reflects itself as infinite beings.**

God is one's own identityless nature of Pure Being.

God is a mirror - like Awareness.

God is space - like Mind or 'Awareness' beyond concepts.

God is one's own self-perception.

God is Pure Being manifesting itself as beings while remaining itself.

God is self cognizing intelligent space.

When we come to examine the nature, attributes and qualities of God, we are forced to use the term potentiality instead of actuality. Although the most accurate translation of the name of God would simply be 'Being' or 'the One who is', since this principle is always individualized, in the sense that we need someone to express it, many spiritual teachings use the term 'I AM'.

'I' because it is individualized but at the same time idenityless (not a separate self being out there), 'Am' because it is always in a state of Being beyond all dualities of birth and death.

However, this should also not cause the confusion of identifying the name of God with some self-entity external to the play of Reality but, on the contrary, we should understand God as the fundamental Expanse of Pure Being, or 'Pure Beingness', a mirror-like all pervading Awareness beyond the limitation of external or internal, one or many, time and space, **residing at the heart of each sentient being.**

From this substantive pure potentiality there flows out an active verb, which reproduces in action, what the 'I AM' is in essence, creation is in essence the same as what has started the creation.

All is Mind, Mind is God - All is God

The meaning of the metaphysical aphorism 'All is Mind - Mind is All' is that the Universe is alive and aware, **the Universe is the effulgence of Pure Being as self - perception.**

If all is a manifestation of Awareness of Pure Being, one's nature, then all forms, energy, motion and power are manifestations of vital-mental action and consequently there is no force but vital-mental force, no energy but vital-mental energy, no motion but vital-mental motion and no power but vital-mental power.

This explanation is directly opposed to the materialistic and nihilist theories which make matter the dominant factor in life in the Universe.

In fact, according to this axiom, in and around everything, and in the very essence of everything resides the 'Knowledge of the Universe' latent within itself (and oneself) and in which in its very presence it exemplifies the capacity of filling all space with mental - energy potentiality.

In the great ocean of one's Awareness, bodies of substance are but as floating bubbles formed of the substance of Being itself. **All is a manifestation of pure mental - energy - potentiality indivisible and non dual from one's own essential nature.**

About God's name

'When you have lifted up the Son of man, then you will realize that I Am'.

John 8:28

The word 'Ehyeh' is used in many places in the Hebrew Bible, where it is often translated as 'I will be' or 'I shall be' as is the case for its final occurrence in Zechariah 8:8.

The original four letters expressing the name of God are ‏י ה ו ה‎ transliterated as the Latin letters 'YHWH', most likely pronounced 'Yahweh' and are derived from a verb that means 'to be', so the most likely translation would be **'the One who is'**.

In the Hellenistic Greek literature of the Jewish Diaspora the phrase 'Ehyeh asher ehyeh' was rendered in Greek as 'Ego eimi ho on' or 'I am Being'.

This divine name is mysterious because it is at the same time the revelation of a name and something like the refusal of a name, and hence it is better to express God as 'what or who always is', infinitely beyond everything that we can understand conceptually, simply ineffability.

A God who reveals its name as the 'I Am', reveals itself as the God who is always there present at the heart of all beings waiting to be recognized and known individually.

Christ too reveals that He bears God's name in John 8:28: *'When you have lifted up the Son of man, then you will realize that "I Am"'.*

About God's qualities

Just like the natural flavour of sugar is sweet, the 'natural flavour' of Awakening to one's nature is non conceptual Wisdom, Love and Compassion.

Our nature of Pure Being has infinite qualities but we can summarize them as four main spontaneous qualities:

- Total freedom from causes and circumstances.
- Infinite wisdom including the clear and complete knowledge of all events and meanings of the three times of past, present and future.
- Infinite love and compassion.

- Total bliss.

When we let ourselves rest and integrate our existence in our nature of Pure Being (which is at the heart of ourselves), we familiarize and manifest these spontaneous qualities in increasing levels and degrees until a state of totally pure energy potentiality beyond all time and space is actualized for oneself and manifested in form for the benefit of all other beings.

God's essential innermost aspect may be characterized as '*power or potentiality*', from this follows the second inner aspect, '*the word*', and from both of these follows the third aspect as '*motion or manifestation*'. This creative triad is the life, the light, and the breath as the source of all things and beings.

The absolute state of resting in Pure Being, one's nature, is beyond any intellectual understanding or description since any description would imply limitation.

On how God manifests itself as one's self perception of reality

The timeless Awareness always present at the heart of oneself is a primordially potentiality which, by breaking free from its formless latency, comes to manifest as an array of light forms which compose an objective field of experience wherein it can now experience itself and become the player of its own dream-like play or drama through infinite 'illusory beings' as mirror images.

This dream - like self appearing play was not started at some point in the past, but it is an ongoing timeless movement which has its root in the timeless 'internal' potentiality of Pure Being itself. An illustration could be an infinite calm ocean (timeless and infinite potentiality) and its perpetual motion of waves (self manifestation as self perception).

If the play of the self manifestation is recognized as simply self perception, one's own adornment, then there is dissolution of seemingly separate cognitions into primordial timeless Expansion as an ongoing experience beyond the division of one and many or past and future or any other conceptual elaboration entailing opposites.

On the other hand, there is a possibility of not recognizing this play of phenomena as one's self perception of Pure Being, in which case, cognition of self and other solidifies into a sentient being and therefore the experience of objective reality, time and space, one and many.

Moreover, since each and every being is a reflection of indivisible mirror - like Awareness of Pure Being, this manifestation from an inner potentiality to a dream - like illusory manifestation happens for every being again and again in the transition from death and re-birth, although completely unrecognized.

God, being simply the potentiality of Pure Being, a mirror - like and all pervading potentiality of energy and Awareness is free to the extent of letting itself not recognize its own self manifestation as self perception in a kind of play of illusory reality.

About the Liberation in the Kingdom of God

'Now when He was asked by the Pharisees when the kingdom of God would come, He answered them and said, "The kingdom of God is not something that can be observed" nor will they say, "See here!' or "See there!", for indeed, the kingdom of God is within you'.

Luke 17:20-21

Almost anybody can find God's perfection in the beautiful and the joyful, but a few realized ones can find perfection in everything including the difficult and 'hellish' experiences of life and death.

This is because true perfection or the Kingdom of God is one's own nature of timeless Awareness beyond any relative conditions of good and evil.

There are also different levels and degrees of Liberation in the Kingdom of God depending on the spiritual evolution of each living being. **This is equivalent to the degree of familiarization with one's own nature of Pure Being and its effulgence as self perception.**

In reality, everything including the outer world and the living beings contained therein are always one's own perception of Pure Being as God here and now without the need to modify anything.

In Matthew 5:3 Jesus says: *'Blessed are the poor in spirit, for theirs is the kingdom of heaven'*. What is the meaning of 'poor in spirit' in this sentence?

The simple but profound joy of Being, recognizing the timeless Awareness that is there when you let go of the various identifications with the ego grasping personality means that you become 'poor in spirit'. This is why renouncing all possessions has been an ancient spiritual practice in both East and West as a symbol of renouncing one's grasping to an ego - identity.

In the ancient Christian traditions, there is a clear distinction between the outer Christ and the inner Christ within. According to these traditions, the Christ within is regarded as the true 'saviour' who needs to be born within each individual in order to evolve toward the Kingdom of God, that is, toward the 'new heavens and a new earth' or the New Galilee.

The second coming or Advent of the Christ is not in a physical body, but in the Awareness of Pure Being of each individual.

In a nutshell the Kingdom or realm of God is one's own nature of Pure Being waiting to be recognized as self perception.

'Don't you know that you yourselves are God's temple and that God's Spirit dwells in your midst?'

Corinthians 3:16

On God's gender

God's essential nature and the essential nature of all its adornment an all pervading Awareness, a potentiality of Pure Being is beyond any gender of male and female.

However, God's endless spontaneous manifestations appear and manifest on a relative illusory level of perceived reality as both pure and 'impure' energy adornments in time and space according to the Principle of Gender of male and female.

The immutable Laws of reality: the Principle of Gender

The Principle of Gender explains the truth that there is gender in everything that is manifested in the Universe; the masculine and feminine principles are present and active in all phases of the manifestation of the play of Reality and on every plane of phenomenal existence. The feminine aspect is the energy manifestation aspect and the masculine aspect is the awareness aspect of the Space of Pure Being.

The word gender here has a much broader and more general meaning than the term sex, since the latter refers only to the physical manifestation of male and female living beings and is just one manifestation of the Principle of Gender on the physical plane of organic life. The Principle of Gender, on the other hand, is responsible for the creating, producing, generating and manifesting phenomena on every plane of reality.

One example is in the physical world, where science tells us that the atom is composed of a dense central nucleus composed by a mix of positively charged protons and neutral neutrons surrounded by a cloud of negatively charged electrons. Sometimes we can find the masculine principle identified with the positive pole and the feminine with the negative pole of energy and this may give rise to confusion. The so-called negative pole is really the pole in and by which the generation or production of new energy is manifested, therefore there is nothing 'negative' about it, on the contrary, we can consider it the mother principle of the manifestation of energy on all levels of self- perceived reality.

The function of the masculine principle is that of directing energy toward the feminine principle, and thus starting into activity the creative processes, but it is the feminine principle the one doing the active creative work and this is observed on all planes of self-perceived phenomena.

Arising from the operation of the Principle of Gender on the plane of material energy, all the phenomena of light, heat, electricity, magnetism, attraction, repulsion and chemical affinity are manifested. **The law of gravity is also another manifestation of the Principle of Gender, which operates in the direction of attracting the masculine and the feminine energies to each other through the 'strings of attraction'.**

Neither the masculine nor the feminine is capable of operating energy without the assistance of the other, and in general all forms of life manifest both genders in different levels and degrees. For example each female human being contains male elements and vice versa. In some forms of life, the two principles are also combined in the same organism in even levels and degrees.

Even though one's nature of Pure Being is beyond any Gender, its manifestation, which is the mental consciousness of a living being, operates through the Principle of Gender.

According to the Principle of mental Gender, one's self-manifesting individual consciousness operates on the basis of a masculine aspect which for convenience we can call the 'I' and a feminine aspect which for convenience we can call the 'Me' operating in unison.

According to this principle, the feminine 'Me' is the part of consciousness in which thoughts, ideas, emotions, feelings, desires and intuitions may be generated. It can be considered as the 'mental womb' capable of generating a mental offspring. This feminine part of consciousness brings with it a realization of an enormous capacity for mental work and creative ability. But even though its powers of creative energy are enormous it seems that it must receive some form of direction from either its own masculine 'I' companion, or else from some other external mental 'I' to produce its mental creations.

The masculine 'I' on the other hand is able to will the feminine 'Me' aspect giving it a kind of direction and purpose and it is also able to stand aside and witness its mental creations. **These two aspects could also be called the 'the feminine emotive pole', manifesting desire, feelings, emotions and intuitions and the 'masculine motive pole' manifesting will power in order to move, concentrate, restrain, control and act.**

The tendency of the mental feminine principle is always in the direction of receiving impressions, while the tendency of the masculine principle is always in the direction of giving them out.

The feminine principle is responsible for the work of generating new thoughts, concepts, ideas, including the work of imagination and intuition. The masculine principle contents itself with the work of willing and directing, and yet without the active help of the masculine principle, the feminine principle could become content with generating mental images which are sometimes the result of impressions received from the will of other minds, instead of producing original mental creations.

I cannot overstress that both males and females sentient beings operate through both mental genders and neither of them can function without the other counterpart.

The normal mode of operation for both the masculine and feminine mental principles is to co-ordinate and act harmoniously in unison, but unfortunately sometimes the masculine mental principle becomes too lazy with the consequence that one can become easily ruled and 'hypnotized' by the minds and wills of others, accepting thoughts and ideas instilled into the 'Me' from the 'I' of others. The reason for this is that mental influence and suggestion operates along the lines of the feminine desire force and masculine will power employed generally in combination.

On the real meaning of the 'original sin'

'You will not certainly die, the serpent said to the woman. For God knows that when you eat from it your eyes will be opened, and you will be like God, knowing good and evil'.

Genesis 3:4-6

In this passage the Principle of Polarity, which will be discussed later, is introduced with the knowledge of good and evil.

The Bible is a book of symbols, in which the inner and secret meaning is always hidden within symbols sometimes difficult to unravel.

On the one hand we find the serpent, which by changing its skin and taking on a new physical appearance, symbolizes the force of the sphere of material existence in contrast with the purely spiritual existence of light. It also symbolizes transformation and , impermanence and continual renewal of life. The woman, on the other hand, is a symbol representing the moving and active aspect and energy function of one's effulgence of Pure Being (and not a female living being).

To paraphrase this story we could say that our 'primal ancestors' of pure light energy potentiality, lived in perfect harmony as God's pure potentiality, fully integrated into the fabric of their latent dimension, there was no need to neither ponder experiential options nor make decisions. They did not yet have a sense of being separate and distinct entities, standing neither apart from their surrounding environment nor from their Primordial source and nor from each other, but also didn't yet 'recognize their face' as the space of Awareness of Pure Being.
Their timeless experience was full and complete, and without any trace of lack, they were without self grasping and also without self realization. Not a word was spoken, nor a gesture made on behalf of a self-centred me.

When they ate from the tree of the knowledge of good and evil, not recognizing their mirror–like nature of Pure Being, they abruptly entered the world of self and other, like and dislike, pleasure and pain, time and space. They gained the capacity to stand back from experience and create concepts in their minds, but lost their child-like innocence and spontaneity. Standing out and apart from the environment, and even from themselves, they experienced self grasping, alienation and sorrow. **This was the birth of time, identity, personality, choice and its consequences, and the Law of Cause and Effect.**

The birth and development of self-grasping and identity marked alienation from Primordial Being itself, one's inherent nature. Once we separated from one's essential nature they created an observer in here, and an observed world out there, and therefore inadvertently created a psychological abyss.

The Christian religion tells us that Christ (the anointed one) was the son of God and without original sin; in reality, what is meant by this affirmation is that Christ recognized himself to be non - dual with God (all embracing Awareness of pure Being) and therefore without sin (non recognition of oneself as indivisible from the nature of Reality and Being).

Since God's potentiality of Pure Being, a mirror - like all pervading Awareness, is in constant spontaneous manifestation beyond time and space, within the total freedom and majesty of this play of effulgence lays the intrinsic opportunity to stray into the duality of opposites without recognizing one's own identityless nature, this being the birth of the 'original sin'.

The 'original sin' is simply the non recognition of oneself as indivisible from God (timeless Awareness), or the not knowing of oneself as a mirror of Pure Being (timeless Awareness).

Within and by the all pervading mirror-like Awareness of Pure Being, an array of illusory forms are self manifested as a spontaneous play of light energy, and given the free opportunity to either self recognition as self manifestation beyond all opposites (including good and evil), and therefore the possibility to freely partake of this infinite play of creation without the illusory division of subject and object, or, otherwise, non recognition and the subsequent limitation into a dimmed awareness of an identified consciousness and the forming of tightly grasped dualistic concepts of opposite value.

God, as an identityless all pervading intelligent potentiality is free to the extent of letting itself not recognize its own manifestation as the play of reality as self manifestation.

In a nutshell, the original sin is both a symptom of our disconnection from our Primordial Source, as well as our confused search to recover it in all the wrong places.

On the true nature of the devil

The term 'devil' comes from the Greek word Διάβολος, diábolos, which means 'to divide' or 'the one who divides'. **In essence, the devil is what divides reality into a subject that interacts with an object and all that this implies.**

The root and the nature of the devil and all the worlds of evil destinies is none other than God's infinite potentiality of identityless Pure Being which does not recognize its own nature as completely beyond relative good and evil.

In its general aspect is the possibility of not recognizing oneself as an identityless and timeless Awareness of Pure Being and the subsequent grasping at identities and all dualities or opposites.

In its individual aspect the devil is the symbol or 'personification' of sentient beings self- grasping at identities and their dualistic conceptual limitations along with all the negative intentions and actions that sprout because of that limitation and ignorance.

Its number, the triple six revealed in the Bible, is the repetition (dualistic limitation) of the three indivisible aspects of God: the Father, the Holy Spirit and the Son, or the Potential, the Ideal and the Concrete or the Essence, the Nature and the Manifestation. **The triple number three is multiplied by two to symbolize the falling into dualistic limitations.**

In final analysis the devil in both its general and individualized aspect is also an indivisible reflection of Pure Being, inseparable from God and indispensable for directing sentient beings in the direction of self - recognition and self - realization as God's adornment.

God is real power. If you refuse that power which is within you refuse God and you end up accepting a miserly shadow of power from the 'dualizing' and dualistic devil.

Chapter 2

About the true nature of sentient beings

'So God created mankind in his own image, in the image of God he created them; male and female he created them'.

Genesis 1:27

Sentient beings are indivisible from God

'For in him we live and move and have our being'.

Acts 17:28

The great 'hidden' truth which has never been taught to the multitudes, being only revealed to a few initiates, is that God and living beings are non dual and that all phenomena is an identityless and timeless non duality.

All that there is, including living beings, is nothing other than idenityless Pure Being 'thinking' itself into diversity.

In oneness all things lose their individual characteristics, whereas as a non duality everything and everyone is simply at the same time individual and without identity, as non separate from everything and everyone else. **In this space of Pure Being singularity and plurality are completely overcome in identityless Awareness where a space- like individuality is maintained.**

We live within a space-like Mind or Awareness which has the capacity to spontaneously 'think itself' into a diversity of apparent forms which in turn might 'freeze' into solidly grasped living beings.

It is not as if God, Pure Being cannot manifest itself as relative evil; God is an infinite energy potentiality which can and does manifest timelessly. Its own co-emergent non recognition and the subsequent grasping at individual identities create the conditions for relative good and evil to be experienced. **Its 'absolute goodness' comes from the fact that whatever is perceived is idenityless, illusory and without any reference or essential reality but simply its own timeless self perception.**

Pure Being lets itself dream into infinite self grasped 'avatars' which are indivisible from itself, and which are endowed with the freedom to act as if they were separate entities capable of choosing between relative good and evil actions.

Pure Being, a great ocean of all pervasive Mind potentiality has its centre everywhere and its circumference nowhere.

This all pervasive potentiality is filled and pervaded with an infinite number of centres of energy, where each dynamic individual being is such a centre for himself or herself, a 'centre of living Will, and each one has the whole Universe circling and revolving around him/her as a self perception. To symbolize this relationship between Being and beings some spiritual teachings employ the symbol of a circle with a dot in the middle.

Some beings are the centres of a tiny dimension, and some have huge dimensions revolving around them. There are centres so expanded and exalted that the human mind cannot grasp, but even the tiniest point of activity is a centre in itself and for itself. **Pure Being and an infinite number of beings are integrated beyond any finite conceptual logic of one and many.**

This Absolute Principle also entails that infinite space and all contained therein is occupied by an all pervasive Awareness pulsating with life and energy, in the depths of which there is a timeless calm and on the surface of which are waves, currents and whirlpools pulsating in rhythmic fashion.

As far as space extends there is an infinite Principle of Being and an infinite number of beings to fill this vast expanse of Awareness. Each dynamic individual being is the centre and the totality of the infinite Universe revolving around him or her. Although no example can fit the description of Reality, one possible example could be an ocean, an infinite body of water, where water is 'the totality' and at the same time, 'infinitely individualized' in each water molecule.

The nature of Pure Being is omnipresent, all penetrating wisdom pervading the entire Universe, occupying all space, and being essentially the same in kind at every point of its presence. Each individual being is essentially the centre of this omnipresent Awareness. This universal potentiality simply is and can manifest only through the individual, just as the individual can manifest only through the universal as in essence they are one.

Each living being is a self reflection of the uncreated, all pervading pure and lucid Expanse of Being which can recognize itself through its own naked Awareness.

In a nutshell, we should think of ourselves as spiritual beings, inhabiting 'timeless eternity', and living in a spiritual Universe, governed by spiritual laws. Even though we cannot alter these laws to suit our own personal convenience, we can work in harmony with them, so that more joy, harmony and peaceful conditions can manifest in our life.

'I and the Father are one'.

John 10:30

On the manifestation of thoughts

'You, as Pure Being, are the potentiality of all events that are happening in your life'.

Hermetic axiom

Modern science thinks of energy purely as a 'mechanical thing' or as something derived from the common forms of energy, such as heat, light or electricity. This limited point of view ignores the fact that one's nature as Pure Being has a 'subtle energy' which it uses to perform its work of manifesting 'outer phenomena' and 'inner conceptual thinking'.

This 'subtle energy' is the cause of any thinking process since thought is as much a form of energy as it is the pulling of a train of cars, and it produces a definite amount of heat resulting from the activity of the fine substance of the brain. Science has taken all of this to mean that thinking is purely a material process and a function of the brain.

It is commonly accepted that it is the matter of the brain doing the thinking instead of considering that mind uses the brain as a substratum or the 'machinery' for the production of thoughts.

The mind is constantly emitting or projecting these subtle particles of 'thought energies' at a distance and rate of speed which is determined by the 'subtle energy' used in their production, there being a great difference between the thought of a concentrated mind, and the one emanating from a confused mind.

These projections of 'thought energies' have a tendency to mingle with the mind of other beings with a corresponding rate of vibration (depending upon the character of the thoughts emitted). Some of these thoughts remain around the places where they were emitted, while others float off and around like clouds and through the Principles of Cause and Effect and Vibration are drawn to human beings or other living beings thinking along similar lines. The characteristic vibration and different atmosphere of different places arises according to the thoughts of their inhabitants causing a corresponding thought vibration to hang over and around it. This is usually felt by visitors and often determines the mental character of the people residing in such places.

Each person draws to himself these particles of vibrating 'thought energies' which correspond to the general mental attitude and vibration occupying his or her mind.

If one harbours ill feelings like hatred, envy and malice, one will find corresponding situations and like minded people holding thoughts of malice, revenge, and hatred. One will have made himself a centre of attraction of such vibrations through the Principles of Reality.

On the other hand, vibrations energized by intense and positive thoughts and which are sent out with such intensity and 'positiveness' that they are almost 'made real', would manifest almost the same degree of mental influence that would have been manifested by the sender if he were present physically.

Much has been written in recent years regarding the 'drawing power of the mind' or 'the Law of Attraction' and although some of what has been written is only a partial understanding of self-perceived reality, there remains a strong base of truth regarding how human beings do attract to themselves success and failure according to the Laws of Reality.

The precise workings of these Laws are somewhat complex to explain in details, but it remains a fact that all of us are constantly ruled by them, consciously or unconsciously according to our dominant mental atmosphere, drawing to ourselves that which we desire or fear the most (see also my book 'The Seen Laws of Reality and Being' for an accurate description of these laws).

The manifestation of worlds, thoughts and emotions: 'the zero point field'

According to the quantum field theory, the vacuum state is the quantum state with the lowest possible energy; it contains no physical particles, and it is the energy of the ground state.

But a vacuum is not really empty even if there are no particles, because there are still fields. The vacuum energy is simply the energy that fields have when they are in the vacuum state. This is also called the zero point energy; the energy of a system at a temperature of zero.

However, even though this is a state of lowest energy is not a state of 'no energy'. There is some amount of energy that the field always has, even when it is in the ground state. This energy is called the vacuum energy or 'zero-point field'.

Since empty space is not empty at all and the vacuum is actually a plenum, there is a cosmic dance of energy back and forth between the physical realm and the zero point field manifesting as constant creation, expansion and dissolution.

Thoughts, emotions and even matter and living beings manifest from this state of pure potentiality without interruption and can be viewed 'dualistically' as a subject interacting with an object or 'non-dualistically' as manifesting from oneself as an adornment of primordial space of Pure Being.

More on how to deal with thoughts and emotions will be explained in chapter 4.

Chapter 3

About the origin and the nature of suffering

The fall into the dualism of opposites

'"You will not certainly die" the serpent said to the woman. "For God knows that when you eat from it your eyes will be opened, and you will be like God, knowing good and evil"'.

Genesis 3:4-6

God has given you, along with an infinite number of sentient beings, non separate reflections of itself, the freedom to either recognize yourself as Pure Being or to not recognize yourself and thereafter the ability to project and individually self perceived reality which you then share with other beings with a similar mindset according to the universal Laws of Reality.

This separation is, however, illusory and self created. There has never been and will never be any real separation, just like space cannot be separated from space. Living beings and God are a space-like omnipresent and timeless Awareness of Pure Being and therefore inseparable.

Pure Being, as pure energy potentiality beyond time and space, as it manifests itself timelessly, remains open to the real possibility of not recognizing 'its own face', and therefore the possibility to create the conditions for the self-grasping at self – perceived identities.

This, however, doesn't mean that Pure Being is a singular entity and sentient beings are plural entities. The dualistic modality of one and many is completely overcome in the

33

recognition Reality. The dualistic framework of an ego-subject experiencing entity-objects is mind made illusion, like free flowing water solidified into ice.

On the nature of suffering

'Man is God afraid'.

Maurice Maeterlinck

The reason we suffer is because we grasp at an illusory separate identity experiencing its own pure energy manifestations as 'other' and we create a self perceived vision of reality veiled by whatever concept we might have.

This process starts within the timelessness of Pure Being and continues infinitely through an uninterrupted succession of lifetimes experience individually.

At the personal level of this unbroken chain of lifetimes, we find the grasped 'I' personality, conditioned, restricted, bound and hampered by the accumulated sheath of causes and effects to the extent of even doubting its own real nature as immutable Pure Being.

The idea of separateness has crept in and the grasped 'I' has failed to realize that it is identical in nature and substance with the great Primordial Potentiality, in which it is a centre or focal point.

We are so entangled in the bonds of identity and personality, so deluded by the illusions of the 'John' or 'Mary' characteristics that we imagine to be 'a someone' apart from some 'others'.

This process of identity clinging at a seeming separateness goes on interrupted life after life unless one becomes conscious of one's own ' face' of Awareness of Pure Being and rests within that recognition as an immutable experience.

Once we have established an ego-clinging habit we start living within the domain of certain natural Laws like the Law of Cause and Effect and the Law of Vibration which shape our lives in a positive or negative way. **Even thought primordially and ultimately each and everyone is already an immutable space of Pure Being, provisionally because of the lack of this knowledge, we are confused into the illusion of identities and wrong views.**

And even though self-grasping is what generates the alienation and suffering in one's life, one needs not to deny or fight this illusion, but rather, one needs only to recognize and familiarize with one's nature in order to 'dissolve' in total knowledge the ego-clinging until a state of self-aware timeless Presence is achieved.

Each and every being including the highest angels and the lowest demons is a reflection of self-aware Primordial Being. The stable knowledge of this truth as an ongoing experience liberates you into the Expanse of Reality and removes all suffering including the concept and the suffering of birth and death.

The origin of human beings on earth

According to Buddhist and Hindu knowledge, human beings were originally more similar to gods or angels with subtle bodies made of light and endowed with an almost infinite lifespan.

In this ancient epoch there was no need for food and the earth was not perceived as we perceive it now as solid matter but as an environment made of light. With the passing of time humans developed grosser and grosser forms of attachment to the objects of the senses and therefore they developed genitals and the need to grow food and unite sexually. The earth started to be perceived as solid matter and with the passing of time human beings 'fell' from living like 'gods in heaven' to living a life of extreme suffering.

This is also hinted symbolically in the Bible with the story of Adam and Eve in the Garden of Eden and the falling from the heavens.

The illusion of evil, death, poverty and illness

The self-knowledge of Pure Being entails no such attributes as evil, old age, illness and death, which afflict humanity. **However, its ignorance does entail the possibility of straying into the illusion of evil, old age, illness and death.**

The suffering of birth, old age, illness and death, comes about because of the veils that create the illusion of self-identity separate from the Primordial Source of Pure Being .

Once we grasp to a separated self and we separate from our nature of Pure Being, **even though this separation is a self created illusion**, we nevertheless create the circumstances for all sorts of evil destinies, suffering, poverty illness and death through the workings of precise laws or principles which will be discussed in the next chapters.

The immutable Laws of reality: the Principle of Cause and Effect (Karma)

'As you sow, you shall reap'.

Galatians 6:7

Everything manifested in the Universe and in one's life happens according to unchanging laws, of which the Law of Cause and Effect is the most important, because not only it rules all planes of reality but it is the fundamental law for the arising of different kinds of self- perceived phenomena.

In the Bible, for example, the Law of Cause and Effect is revealed in the statement: *'As you sow, you shall reap' (Galatians 6:7)* where we are introduced to the truth that what one wishes or does to others sooner or later one will experience himself.

In fact nothing ever 'merely happens', and there is no such thing as chance, since a careful examination will show that what we call chance is merely a common expression regarding causes that we cannot perceive or that we cannot understand.

There is an interdependent continuity between all events and also a relation existing between everything that has gone before, and everything that follows after. Every thought we think, everything we say and every act we perform, has its direct and indirect consequence which fits into the great chain of Cause and Effect.

There is usually a time gap between the cause and the subsequent effect which always depends on many secondary conditions in order to manifest.

Sometimes secondary conditions favour the activation of more negative causes to manifest and sometimes they favour more positive causes, but sooner or later all causes will manifest as effects and shape one's life circumstances. In general terms, one can never set any cause in motion without calling forth those effects which it already contains in embryo and which will again become causes in their turn, thus producing a series of causes and effects which will continue to flow on 'ad infinitum' until one bring into operation a cause of an opposite character to the one which originated it or one employs a specific method of counteraction (in the latter case a specific spiritual practice of some kind).

Whenever a primary cause has been planted, just like a seed in a field, if it doesn't meet any hindrances, it is definite that it will bring a result of its kind. Just like a perfect seed surrounded by the right secondary circumstances will take time to ripen, causes take time to manifest as self - perceived reality.

However if the primary cause meets a hindrance, or it is counteracted by a primary cause of an opposite nature then it is possible that it won't bring a result. A clear example of this is the planting of a seed in a fertile ground, which, even though it has the ability to grow, there is always the chance to disturb the conditions that cause the seed to produce its fruit, for example by taking the seed out or to burn it, or by pouring hot water over it etc.

For a complete primary cause to be set in motion we always need four factors: the basis of the action or the object at which the action is aimed, the intention to act based on a motivation which can be positive, negative or neutral, the action itself needs to be carried out directly or indirectly, and afterward we need to be satisfied or at least feel no regret.

'The pure potentiality of Being is beyond time, space and beyond any laws, but its own manifestation is always governed by unchanging laws'.

The most common question people have in general about Cause and Effect is why some sentient beings seem to commit all sorts of negative actions while living a seemingly comfortable and healthy life and some others which dedicate themselves to many virtuous actions, especially spiritual in kind, seem to suffer from all sorts of obstacles.

The answer to this has many aspects: the first aspect is that Cause and Effect is not some kind of 'justice maker' which sits there and decides who is to get what kind of punishment for this or that action.

The second aspect is that, causes ripen and manifest into a specific effect or chain of effects only when the secondary circumstances are conducive for this to happen regardless of the passing of time, whether it will be a minute or a million years; for example if one has planted many causes for the manifestation of wealth by being selflessly generous, the effect will manifest when certain specific circumstances act as secondary causes for that specific primary cause or causes to be activated and manifest.

And third, and most important, Cause and Effect sometimes tends to manifest a kind of 'karmic flood' for some beings which indulge in extremely positive or negative intending actions. This manifests in a way in which one tends to 'use up' all positive or negative store of primary causes while engaging in a virtuous or non virtuous lifestyle.

In other words, someone committing a great deal of negative intending deeds might experience a great deal of positive circumstances and therefore 'use up' all meritorious causes with the consequence of ending up later on in the most distressful life circumstances and environment for a very long time and many lifetimes.

On the opposite side, someone who is engaging in skilful and virtuous activities, and especially of a spiritual kind, might experience all sorts of mildly negative circumstances in order to consume all residual negative primary causes until the total consummation of all negative causes.

This is why one should never envy or compare oneself with pride or shyness to other beings, since nobody knows what is going to happen next, which causes one has planted or are about to ripen.

In most cases, and for most of us in the human dimension, because of their depending on specific secondary circumstances for their ripening, Causes and Effects manifest in a more mixed kind of fashion alternating 'good and bad' circumstances in one's self-perception.

On how primary Causes manifest Effects

According to a hadith (a divine utterance), Allah said, 'O My servants, it is but your deeds that I reckon up for you and then recompense you for'.

There are three general rules regarding the ripening of Causes as Effects:

- **The first is the certainty of the result**, which means that unless it meets a hindrance or one purifies a negative action, or neutralize it with a positive action of the same nature and weight, the result will never disappear until the right circumstances for its ripening present themselves. Connected to this is the fact that the passing of time does not wear off primary causes. But even though infinite causes have been planted, there is always the chance to change them or not to experience their result by completely purifying or counteracting them with a primary set of causes of an opposite nature, which is like destroying the ability of seeds to grow.

- **The second rule of ripening is the increase of the result** which means that from a small action very large results can follow.
- The third is that **if one has not committed a certain action, one will not experience its results** even if the secondary circumstances present themselves, although one would still experience the effect of planned actions which he didn't actually commit in person, but told someone else to do, like for example paying someone to kill someone etc.

Effects can manifest in various ways and these can include feeling a level of happiness or unhappiness in one's life, experiencing a specific rebirth state and a specific environment like being born in a clean place or a dirty place, experiencing being born with a specific nationality and so on.

Another effect that comes from specific primary causes is a compulsive feeling or desire to act in a similar way to how one has acted before. The effect is that we would like to act in such a way and we want to do it again and again. Whether or not we pay attention to this feeling as something worthwhile to act out depends on many other variables, not the least of which are the external circumstances we are in.

Experiencing the feeling may or may not bring about the arising of an impulse to repeat that action, and the impulse to repeat it may or may not lead to actually repeating it, but if the impulse arises, that impulse will produce further causes.

Another result is the experiencing of something similar to what we did before, but now happening back to us. For example, we were always complaining to people and now we are always meeting people who complain back to us.

Finally, our perception of things is very limited or 'periscopic', we cannot really see why someone acted in a certain way or what the consequences of our actions will be. We are constantly producing and experiencing this limited 'periscopic' perception.

It is all very complex because the results of primary causes are constantly going up and down, in one moment we are happy, in the next we are unhappy, now this happens and now that happens, now we feel like doing this and now we feel like doing that.

While our experiences are going up and down, we also experience a limited vision of reality; we don't really understand what is going on or what is going to happen next.

The four ways of ripening into effects

- The first is **the effect of maturation**, the experience of one's birth aggregates, like the type of body and mind or intelligence one has, and the particular dimension in which one has been reborn.
- The second is **the effect in agreement with the cause in the action**, which is the urge or compulsion in every moment to intend and do something similar to what we did before and experience its effects.
- The third is called **the conditioning effect** which can be related to the environment in which we are born and in that rebirth, all the various feelings of happiness and unhappiness we experience.
- The fourth is **the effect in agreement with the cause in the experience or the cumulative effect of ripening,**

which is the tendency to experience a situation similar to what we did, with the same situations happening back to us over and over, (we kill once and we are killed sequentially many times), **one cause can ripen into many effects.**

Sometimes a differentiation is also made between **'throwing and completing causes'**. The former being the causes that have the potentiality to 'throw' us into the next rebirth, and the latter being the ones responsible for shaping our life, for example we can be reborn as a dog due to the 'throwing causes', but then depending on the 'completing causes' we could be either a stray dog in constant search for food or a pet in some rich household.

On reincarnation

"Even though we are 'individually 'a Space of Pure Being, we must go beyond grasped identities".

Hermetic Axiom

Although the Law of Cause and Effect is mainly described in the Eastern spiritual traditions, early Christians believed in the transmigration of souls before the second council of Constantinople in A.D. 553 declared it a heresy.

The Jews might have been familiar with the principle of rebirth or they would not have asked John the Baptist if he were Elijah, as recorded in the first chapter of John.

Christ's Apostles also might have held the belief of rebirth as we may see from the incident recorded in Matthew 16:14 where Christ asked them the question: *'Who do men say that I the Son of Man am'?* And the Apostles replied: *'Some say that Thou art John the Baptist; some, Elias; and others Jeremiahs or one of the Prophets'.*

Other instances asserting the concept of rebirth can be found in John 3:3 where Christ says: *'Except a man is born again, he* cannot *see the kingdom of God'*, and in Matthew 11:14, speaking of John the Baptist Christ says: *'This is Elijah.'* And again in Matthew 17:12 Christ says: *'Elijah has already come, and they did not recognize him, but have done to him everything they wished, then the disciples understood that he spoke to them of John the Baptist'.*

Thus the understanding of rebirth offers the only solution to the inequalities of existence in harmony with the laws of nature. Rebirth also answers the ethical requirements that permit us to love all beings without blinding our reason to the inequalities of life and the varying circumstances which give to a few the ease, comfort and health, that are denied to the many.

The principle of rebirth, which is in essence the same as the Law of Cause and Effect, shapes our lives because our birth and circumstances are determined by the manner in which we lived before.

The gambler is drawn to race tracks to associate with others of like taste, the musician is attracted by the concert halls and music studios and in each case the returning 'grasped identity' also carries with it its likes and dislikes which cause it to seek parents and companions among the class to which it belongs.

But then someone will point to cases where we find people of entirely opposite attitudes living lives of torture in the same family and forced by circumstances to stay there contrary to their wills.

This is made possible by the fact that the two who have injured each other in previous lives may find themselves members of the same family. Then, the old enmity will assert itself and cause them to hate each other again at first until the consequent discomfort forces them to tolerate each other, and perhaps later on they may learn to love each other.

One may also ask why if we have been here before do we not remember the events of past lives. The answer is that since our experience is an illusion created by the non recognition of the timeless Nature of Pure Bering, similar to what we experience in a dream, we lack the clarity of perfect memory in just the same way don't remember last night's or last week's or last month's dreams

43

in their entirety, especially after having experienced the trauma of birth and death.

The immutable Laws of reality: The Principle of Vibration

'In the beginning was the Word, and the Word was with God, and the Word was God'.

John 1:1

In this citation 'Word' stands for vibration and sound, and in this case sound is the essence of Pure Being, or we could say the energy of Pure Being (God) in the general and individualized aspects, able to start a sequence of creation, whether in the large cosmic scale or in the microcosmic plane of self perceived phenomena.

The Principle of Vibration tells us that everything, from the totality of the self perceived universe to the heart of each sentient being and down to the grossest form of matter, all is in motion and everything vibrates. The higher the vibration, the higher the position in the scale and the closer it is to the primal 'causeless' cause of Pure Being.

The Expanse of Pure Being which is at the heart of every living being vibrates at such an infinite rate of intensity and rapidity that it is practically at rest, just as a rapidly moving wheel seems to be motionless. At the other end of the scale, there are grosser forms of matter whose vibrations are so low as to seem at motionless too.

The rate of vibration is like a specific frequency of a particular phenomenon or event in time and space which determines the particularities and characteristics of that event.

For example we think of the sun as giving us light, yet we know it is simply giving forth energy which produces vibrations in the ether causing light waves. Therefore what we call light is simply a form of energy and the only light there is, is the sensation caused in the mind by the motion of the energy waves. When the rate of vibration increases, the light changes in colour, each change in colour being caused by shorter and more rapid vibrations, so that although we speak of the rose as being red, the grass as being green, we know that the colours exist only in our minds and the sensations are the result of the vibrations of light waves. When the vibrations are reduced below a certain speed, they no longer affect us as light, but we experience the sensation of heat.

It is evident, therefore, that everything we experience is simply a manifestation of a different rate of vibration.

On the level of shared perception, what is generally regarded as good or bad luck is really the vibratory 'pushes and pulls' of primary causes activated by the circumstantial vibration of that specific moment which give rise to that specific 'lucky' or 'unlucky' event. Fortune is the positive potential of virtuous primary causes manifesting in time and space as an event due to secondary favourable circumstances, misfortune and bad luck is its opposite.

A thought is a form of energy, and therefore a rate of vibration, but a thought or, more specifically, the 'non-thought' of the Truth of one's nature of Pure Being is the highest rate of vibration and consequently it can dissipate from one's mind every form of negative vibration in exactly the same way that light can instantly dissipate darkness.

The immutable Laws of reality: The Principle of Polarity (or Law of Opposites)

The Principle of Polarity or Law of Opposites states that the play of reality manifests always two sides, or two poles, and the difference between these two seemingly diametrically opposed poles is merely a matter of degree.

According to the Law of Opposites, everything attains completion by manifesting itself in the opposite direction to that from which it started. For example the spiritual and the physical planes are in reality the different poles of the same thing: the play of the Expanse of Pure Being.

This Principle is expressed in the Bible in the passage: *'You will not certainly die' the serpent said to the woman. 'For God knows that when you eat from it your eyes will be opened, and you will be like God, knowing good and evil'. Genesis 3:4-6*

In this passage, we find the Principle of Polarity introduced with the knowledge of good and evil. Since the potentiality of Pure Being, a mirror-like all pervading potentiality of Awareness is in constant spontaneous timeless manifestation, **within the total freedom and majesty of this play of effulgence lays the intrinsic opportunity to stray into the duality of opposites without recognizing their own illusory nature as a self perception.**

Within and by the omnipresent Awareness of Pure Being, an array of illusory light forms are self manifested as a spontaneous play, and given the free opportunity to either self recognition as self manifestation beyond all opposites (including good and evil), and therefore the possibility to freely enjoy of this infinite play of creation without the illusory division of subject and object, or, otherwise, non recognition and the subsequent limitation into a dimmed awareness or consciousness and the forming of tightly grasped dualistic concepts of opposite values.

The knowledge of one's nature of Pure Being includes the knowledge of the play of opposites as good and evil according to the Principle of Polarity as a spontaneous illusory play of self perception.

We suffer because we don't recognize ourselves as an Awareness of Pure Being beyond opposites, already perfect and fulfilled as it is, and we don't recognize its manifestation as a play of ever transforming adornment of self perception.

The immutable Laws of reality: The Principle of Rhythm and Cyclicity

This Principle embodies the truth that everything in the physical, mental and spiritual dimension expresses itself in rhythm from action to reaction, from activity to inactivity with a 'to and from' movement, a flow and inflow, out and in, a swing forward and backward, an advance and a retreat, a rising and a sinking, a giving and a receiving. The very essence of the play of Reality itself is always a spontaneous outpouring and an in drawing of energy and manifestation.

Cyclicity is only a more complex form of rhythm and is dependent on the latter. Cyclicity happens when the action and reaction, the attraction and repulsion, arising from the conflict between the force of the rhythmic swing in a straight line on the one hand, and the attractive and repellent forces from without tend to swing the movement in a perfect circle around a central point of motion manifesting the universal tendency to convert the straight path of the swing into a circular path or cycle.

Proof of this is the movements of small and large bodies in the physical Universe, the planets around the stars, the galaxies around the Universe or the electrons around the atoms which perpetually revolve in a circle around some given centre point continuing in cyclic revolution due to the Principle of Rhythm and Cyclicity and never collapsing toward the centre.

All living things including sentient beings are born, grow, and die, and then are reborn, always completing a full cycle according to the Principle of Cyclicity. And the same applies to all great movements, philosophies, beliefs, fashions, governments, all manifesting birth, growth, maturity, decadence, death and then a new birth. Also in the mind of beings the succession of moods, feelings and other states of consciousness manifest following the Principle of Rhythm and Cyclicity.

Likewise in the macrocosm this continuously occurs as rain that falls, evaporates and goes up, condenses in the sky and falls into a perpetual motion. This process is called circulation because it is a cyclic ascent and descent of the matter, often depicted as a dragon biting its tail, the 'Ouroborus'.

The Ouroboros as a symbol of Cyclicity

The symbol of the 'Ouroboros', or the serpent biting its own tail is first seen around 1600 years BC in Egypt. From there it moved to the Phoenicians and then to the Greeks, who called it the 'Ouroboros', which means *devouring its tail*.

The serpent biting its tail is found in other traditions as well, including the Norse mythology, where the serpent's name is 'Jörmungandr', and in the Hindu tradition, where the dragon circles the tortoise which supports the four elephants that carry the world.

The 'Ouroboros' eating its own tail symbolizes the cyclic nature of the Universe: creation out of destruction, life out of death. It eats its own tail to sustain its life, in an eternal cycle of renewal.

The energy nature of the Universe as a self perception

Primordial Being should be thought as filling all space. Material bodies, like stars and worlds which seem apparently free and unconnected are actually floating in the great Expanse of Pure Being. They are linked together by a web of strings of gravitation; each body of substance has a string reaching out in a continuous direction connecting it with another body.

Each body of substance has countless energetic strings reaching out from it, some slender, and some thick, the thickness depending upon the ratio of distances maintained by, and relative to the sizes of, the particular bodies that it connects to.

This system of energetic strings form a great network of connections in the Expanse of the God (Universe), crossing each other at countless points without interfering with each other.

These energetic strings do not cover the entire dimensions of infinite space, as there are great areas of space entirely untouched by these lines. If one could see the system of energetic strings, it probably would appear as a sheared off section of a great spider's web, with lines in all directions, but with great areas of space between them. Each particle is connected with every other particle in the Universe by a string of attraction.

These 'strings of attraction' are what we call gravitation in modern science and are purely 'mental energy' in nature; they are strings of Mind Principle in the great Expanse of Pure Being.

These energetic strings of gravitation have existed since the creation of the Universe, whether in the macrocosmic or microcosmic worlds.

This Principle reveals the great secret of the fact that no 'time' is required for the passage of gravity, as it seems to be travelling instantaneously, whereas, in fact, it does not 'travel' or 'pass' at all, but it remains constant and ever present between the particles, varying only in degree as the distance between the particles is increased. Increasing and decreasing in effect according to the number of particles combining the lines of attraction.

Gravitation is a mental connection uniting the several particles and bodies in the Universe, and the strings of gravitation are never broken, and could never be, otherwise the particles of substance would be swept out of existence, in which case the balance of the Universe would be broken, and chaos would result.

The desire for attachment between bodies of matter arises from the force of attraction that exists between each particle of substance. The desire for non-attachment arises from some inward inclination for freedom between the same particles.

49

These two desires or inclinations may be called desire for impression and the desire for expression.

The desire for impression (or pressing in) manifests along the lines of action tending toward attraction, companionship and combination. The desire for expression (or pressing out) manifests along the lines of action tending toward individuality, freedom, independence, etc. Both are strong cravings which tend to produce unrest, which results in motion and impermanence.

The 'pull' of the desire of impression is always modified and counteracted by the 'push' of the desire for expression; and, resulting from the play of these two forces, there result activity, motion and change. Like the two conflicting angels in the Persian mythology, Ahriman and Ormuzd, these two desires wrestle with each other in the theatre of the Universe resulting in motion and change.

These conflicting desires for separateness and unity, respectively, are but different forms of the universal desire for wholeness through oneness or non duality.

Impression seeks oneness and wholeness by combination with other separated particles, but cannot find it. Expression seeks oneness and wholeness by drawing apart and endeavouring to realize it in that way, but cannot find it. Both are but different aspects of the same desire for wholeness, and only when we recognize the immutable nature of Pure Being, which is absolute oneness in diversity, does satisfaction and wholeness come, and thus the knowledge of the particles becomes the knowledge of humanity and existence.

The self perception of reality is perfect to the finest detail as every particle is needed, known, and counted in an infinitely balanced Universe.

The different planes of existence

In a multidimensional Universe there are different 'planes of existence' as manifestations of the play of the Expanse of Pure Being which are inhabited by beings which haven't yet realized their timeless nature.

The Hermetic spiritual traditions speak of three different planes or dimensions of Reality:

I.   The great physical planes.
II. The great mental planes.
III. The great spiritual planes.

Each of these planes is divided into seven different sub divisions according to the Law of Vibration and the Law of Cause and Effect.

These ancient spiritual teachings regard matter as a form of energy, that is, energy at a low rate of vibration of a certain kind, therefore the **seven physical planes** include three planes of physical matter and three of energy which ranges from the physical energy (heat, light, magnetism, electricity, and gravity or attraction) to the more spiritual energy used by spiritually developed beings and which may be considered 'divine or miraculous power'.

These seven physical planes are separated by the 'plane of ethereal substance' which is what science calls 'ether', a substance of extreme elasticity, pervading all universal space, and acting as a medium for the transmission of waves of physical energy (such as light, heat, electricity, radio waves etc) and spiritual energy (the phenomena of 'mentation', thoughts etc). This ethereal substance also forms a connecting link between the plane of matter and energy.

The seven mental planes comprise minerals, plants, animals and human beings in ascending order according to the Law of

Cause and Effect, the Law of Vibration and the degree of spiritual development expressed by each of them.

The seven spiritual planes include 'god like' beings possessing life, mind, capacities and forms so exalted compared to the human beings of this era that our mind cannot even conceive. The life and bodies of these beings are 'clothed in pure energy' vibrating at a very high rate due to such positive spiritual causes accumulated in previous lives.

But even the highest of these advanced 'god like' beings exist merely as a 'reflection' of the play and effulgence of Reality, and are still subject to laws as much as human beings or animals on earth. These 'god like' beings are still mortal, even though their life span can last millions of human years, and therefore destined to endless rebirth until the total realization of their intrinsic nature of Pure Being.

The three worlds or planes of existence in Buddhism

Buddhist cosmology shares many similarities with Hindu cosmology in terms of cycles of time and type of beings inhabiting those planes of existence (although the names and details can vary in each tradition), therefore in this chapter I will only describe the Buddhist view of the Universe.

Buddhist cosmology can be divided into three related branches: spatial cosmology, which describes the arrangement of the various dimensions in a vertical pattern and is related to the beings inhabiting that specific Universe; horizontal cosmology which describes how these different dimensions are grouped in the Universe, and temporal cosmology, which describes how the various Universes come into existence, remain and how they pass away.

In spatial cosmology we find an explanation of three planes of existence in ascending order, which are the dimensions of different types of beings according to the Law of Cause and Effect and the

Law of Vibration. What causes a specific dimension and Universe to manifest is the collective primary causes, or the sum of all intending thoughts and emotions (and therefore actions) of all the beings inhabiting that specific dimension.

The three planes of existence in Buddhism are:

    I.   The world of sensuous desire (kāmaloka)
    II.   The world of 'fine matter' or energy (rūpaloka)
    III.   The formless world (arūpaloka)

The **world of desire** comprises eleven dimensions in ascending order which ranges from hell beings to starving wondering spirits, animals, humans and six types of heavenly 'god like' beings. The beings reborn in the world of desire are dominated by attachment to the five sense pleasures and the causes to be reborn in each one of them are virtuous or non virtuous actions committed by body or speech motivated by negative, positive or neutral thought-intentions.

According to the Buddhist view, five types of predominant emotions can become the cause for rebirth as a different type of being in the realm of sensuous desire and these primary causes also shape the 'manifested environment' experienced by the consciousness of that specific being as a shared self perception.

A mind dominated by anger is the cause for rebirth in the dimension of the various hells, predominant greed and attachment causes one to be reborn as a starving spirit, a continuous and dense state of dullness and fogginess of mind and a very dimmed awareness without the ability of discernment of what to accept and what to reject causes the birth as a type of animal, humans are caused by an even mix of different emotions and the accumulation of virtuous intentions and actions (although in the human realm one can also notice all the different degrees of suffering and joy depending on the predominant emotion). Heavenly or 'god like' beings are caused by predominant pride and a great store of accumulated virtuous intentions and actions.

The world of 'fine matter' (or pure light energy) comprises seventeen different planes inhabited by 'deities' possessing extremely refined bodies composed of pure light energy which is invisible to the inhabitants of the worlds of desire. The causes to be reborn in one of these seventeen world dimensions are the attainments of some level of one pointed concentration through meditation, having developed the clarity of discernment, and at the same time having temporarily suppressed the main emotions of greed, attachment, hatred and ill-will.

The formless world is formed by four different planes of 'pure consciousnesses' inhabited by beings without shape or location. The causes to be reborn as one of these formless beings are the meditative absorptions into one of the four different levels of thoughtless trance, transcendental type of meditation, meditating on one's consciousness as infinitely pervasive or meditating on infinite space and infinite nothingness.

Also in Buddhism, all of these different types of 'planes' or 'realms' of existence into which beings can be reborn are considered not beyond the cycle of infinite rebirths and therefore bound by impermanence and the all pervading suffering of existence. The beings born therein have not realized the non dual wisdom potentiality inseparable from 'the Supreme Source' beyond time and space, subject and object and all related dualities.

Chapter 4

How to discover the Principle of Pure Being and how to apply this knowledge in one's perception of reality

How to discover one's nature as Pure Being

God is the spiritual creative principle of the Universe and an all pervading potentiality of Pure Being. Man is made in the image and likeness of God and therefore is a spiritual being indivisible from God and with the same qualities.

The Principle of Pure Being fills the entire Universe, so that all is from it and in it, and there is nothing that is outside of it. Indeed, *'in God we live and move and have our being'*.

The great central fact in human life is the coming into a conscious, vital realization of one's oneness with God as a timeless Space of Pure Being, and the complete familiarization with this sacred realization.

This is the great central fact in human life, for in this all else is included, all else follows in its train. In just the degree that we come into a conscious realization of our indivisibility with God, and open ourselves to this Truth, do we actualize in ourselves the qualities and powers of infinite life intrinsic in this realization.

We can only conceive of God as something always Being, and that's why the name announced to Moses by God was 'the One who is' or the individualized 'I AM'. 'I' because it is always individualized and at the same time selfless (without any self grasped identity), 'Am' because it is always in a state of Being beyond all dualities. **One should not confuse and think that this all pervading pure potentiality is a magnificent and all powerful self-identified principle, but instead one should recognize that** the selfless 'I AM' is a thoughtless Awareness of Pure Being and the central principle which is at the root of all things, it is Life itself.

It is not life in particular forms of manifestation, it is something more essential, it is the 'essential non duality of Being' not yet passed into diversity, **it is a 'non entity' endowed with infinite potentiality of entities**. All individual sentient beings are and remain always inseparable from their selfless and all pervading nature of Pure Being but due to the different concepts of themselves, they are displaying only a limited aspect of this omnipresent potentiality.

One method to experience one's nature is to visualize oneself divested of all thoughts, feelings and identification with the body/mind personality complex, setting aside as the 'not the I' category all attributes and characteristics of self- personality.

By practicing this self-examination, having stripped the ego or the grasped sense of 'I' personality of all possible attributes, it is possible to acknowledge 'a something left', a surd, an irreducible element, an insoluble residuum, **something which, while experienced, is incapable of being described, expressed or designated by rational terms**, a final algebraical 'X', an ultimate timeless, selfless, thoughtless and all pervading element.

This is not an altered state of consciousness like the one that can be achieved through meditation methods employed by some spiritual practitioners (and also described later in this chapter), but simply the pure, unspeakable and essential Awareness of Pure Being beyond thoughts and concepts which is equivalent to all pervading Reality and God itself. It is one's real nature.

Another method is to imagine oneself as rising above the lower planes of personality toward the higher planes of knowledge just like a hot air balloon which is rising above the surface of the earth into the higher regions of pure rarefied air.

Then one should imagine throwing overboard from the balloon all the likes and dislikes, loves and hates, prejudices for and against anything and everything whatsoever, either good or bad; in short the entire collection of inherited or acquired feelings and emotions which have formed the garment of one's personality in this and in previous lives.

As the hot air balloon rises higher and higher, one should throw off even the more subtle feelings and emotions, until finally one finds oneself divested of every iota of personal character ever possessed, one is finally naked just like a new-born baby.

After having done this visualization a few times one will come to a new sense of power, a new realization of one's real nature as Pure Being. Then one will realize that the pairs of opposites and dualities that form one's personality are but masks and clothing of the character one has been playing all along without any true value.

By examining the nature, attributes and qualities of this element of 'Pure Being' we are left with '*a something*' which can be experienced individually **(it is never a mass experience)** but we cannot describe; a timeless, selfless and complete **'individually aware Expanse of Knowledge'** which can only be defined by the term '*potentiality*' or power instead of 'actuality'.

Moreover this newly discovered knowledge never fluctuates into separating events (although one's recognition of it can come and go at first) like the dualistic consciousness which switches on and off according to various circumstances (for example day and night, birth and death etc). **It is an omnipresent and all pervading lucid Awareness of Pure Being beyond concepts and ideas. It is God and it is you at the same time.**

To live undisturbed by passing occurrences you must first find your own centre as Pure Being and be firm in your realization, and so rule the world from within it. You must not surrender this Awareness to nobody and to nothing. In the degree that you do this will you find yourself growing stronger and fearless.

The base of all realizations: meditation and presence

A general definition of concentration or meditation would be *'to bring to a centre'*. Concentration is the undisturbed power of subjective attention over an object of consciousness; therefore concentration is the domain and the best of mind's tools. **Once mastered, concentration is called *presence of mind* and can also serve the purpose of focusing the power or energy of Pure Being for a specific purpose.**

Meditation may be developed by practice and many methods exist in this field. One example is the meditation which focuses on the breath employed by practitioners of Buddhism and Hinduism, in fact the term meditation can sometimes have the same meaning as what in the West is known as concentration, or **we could also say that meditation is the practice to develop undistracted concentration, or undistracted presence of mind.**

After having mastered undistracted concentration with a physical or non physical object (for example a flower or the breath), one's focus of concentration will shift to one's now utterly calm mind or consciousness itself, mind will be concentrating on mind itself, until a state undistracted by any movement of thoughts or emotions is achieved which is then **called *'undistracted presence of mind'*, or the *'abiding in the present moment'*. This doesn't mean that thoughts and emotions are not present but simply that one is not distracted by their movements.**

In a nutshell, the whole process of concentration or meditation consists in fixing the attention upon something which can be physical, non physical, or one's own consciousness itself and being able to hold it there without being distracted by wondering thoughts or emotions.

Once mastered in practice sessions, undistracted meditation is then carried into all daytime activities and then it is called *'undistracted presence of mind'*, or the *'abiding in the present moment'* or, as in the words of Eckhart Tolle, *'the power of Now'*.

Even though this might seem a great spiritual achievement if viewed from an 'ordinary distracted state of mind', it is certainly not the permanent realization of the totally lucid and all pervading Awareness of Pure Being, one's timeless nature beyond space and time and beyond mind.

How to develop mind's presence through meditation

There are many different methods to develop mind's presence, and they all achieve the same purpose.

A simple method would be to hold the mind in a 'one-pointed' way upon an object of attention, which could be a material object like a flower (or anything pleasing to the eyes) or an internal non physical object like the breath for example.

In the case of the breath, one would concentrate in a 'one pointed way' on the inhaling and exhaling process without altering or modifying it. In case one focuses on an external object like a flower instead of the breath, one should be aware that concentration does not mean 'staring' at something but it consists in fixing and holding the mind, not the eyes.

By applying any of these two methods, one will very soon start noticing how many distracting thoughts and emotions can carry one away from the object of meditation. The practice then consists in gently bringing back the mind to the object of meditation over and over again, without following or rejecting the distracting thoughts and emotions, until one is able to effortlessly direct the focalized mental power of concentration upon whatever object, concept or aim without any distractions.

Eventually, after having mastered concentration upon a physical (or non physical object like the breath), one will be able to focus one's concentration upon one's own mind. This entails 'remaining' peacefully present to one's own mind or consciousness while staring into empty space, and in this case mind becomes 'the object' of mind's meditation until a totally peaceful, aware and present state of mind is achieved.

The final result of all these practices is that one is able to carry this new acquired skill of peaceful undistracted presence into all daytime activities and one is able carry out any activity or task with total accuracy and without any effort, without generating resistance to what is manifesting in the present moment.

Regarding this newly acquired skill of undistracted attention and peaceful presence, many spiritual traditions fall into the 'trap' of considering the spacious and calm 'ground consciousness', or 'subconscious mind' as the final aim of their practice and therefore to focus on this spacious consciousness, cultivating a calm, blissful and undistracted state of presence which is then considered a spiritual realization or some form of Enlightenment. In actual fact, although a very important acquired skill, it is certainly not 'the Truth that makes you permanently free', and not the permanent realization of the totally lucid and all pervading Awareness of Pure Being, one's nature beyond space and time and beyond mind.

Nevertheless, since all the following methods of mental imaging, creative visualization, positive statements and methods of prayer are based on the power of undistracted mental presence, the day you achieve control over the movements of your attention, is the day you will acquire the capacity to work creatively with your circumstances and gain control over your life.

Not only, but the power to abide undistracted in the present moment, is an indispensable quality of consciousness if one wants to make any spiritual realization.

How to deal with the habit of distraction

When you realize you have been caught in a thought or an emotion, don't judge or blame yourself as it happens even to the most experienced practitioners of meditation.

Instead of following the thought, as you have done until now, gently shift your attention back to experience the present moment, look at the mind that is generating the thought.

Let your attention rest in that experience of mind itself, don't try to concentrate or hold it there but just bring your attention back to the source of the thoughts and emotions.

The practice is simply learning how to stay present, and how to return to the present moment in any given situation undistracted by the movement of thoughts and emotions.

How to help others through the knowledge of one's nature as Pure Being

'I said, You are gods; all of you are the sons of the Most High'.

Psalms 82:6

The best and foremost way to help others is to see them as they truly are: God-like spiritual beings, just like oneself. Knowing that reflections always manifest the same attributes and qualities of their source, all beings are in fact timelessly the perfect adornment of Pure Being.

Knowing this, if you wish to help someone or wish to develop an attitude of compassion, train in seeing others as already possessing the attributes and qualities of Pure Being, in other words, see them as already possessing wisdom, health, prosperity, intelligence, courage, love and compassion.

The training simply consists in not seeing sentient beings as they seem to be manifesting superficially and temporarily due to their self-grasped personality because of not knowing the Space of Reality, but to see them as they really are in their fundamental nature, embodying God's qualities such as wisdom, love, compassion, health, prosperity, intelligence, accomplishment, fulfilment and fearlessness.

You are not inventing a new harmonious 'reality' as a kind of fantasy, you are just trying to see things as they really are; the intrinsic harmony within and between all phenomena.

Also the Buddha said in the Prajnaparamita Sutra: *'Not just Enlightened Beings but all the structures of relativity are dwellers in the boundlessness which constitutes the all-embracing love, selfless compassion, sympathetic joy and blissful equanimity'.*

Pure self-perception is never something that happens in the future, but an actuality of the ever present here and now of one's mind.

Therefore if you wish to help someone who is suffering an illness, the best would be to see that being as healthy; in case of poverty see abundance and prosperity; instead of frustration and loneliness see accomplishment, fulfilment and love, **basically try to see the Truth hidden behind the veil of temporary adventitious circumstances**. If this is too difficult at first, the best is to create a mental image of the person you are trying to help possessing these perfect qualities, knowing that the visualized image is a *'fac simile'* of the Truth of Pure Being.

Of course this does not mean that one should become uncaring or cold hearted, thinking that everyone is already perfect why bother to say or do anything for others. On the contrary one should carry out all possible helping activities concretely for the benefit of others respecting the Law of Cause and Effect, while, at the same time and without contradiction, having the awareness of the perfection of all living beings.

One should always remember that no matter what the difficulty is, no matter where it is, no matter who is affected,

there is no 'patient' but oneself, or one's own mind, and therefore, one has to convince only oneself of the Truth which one desires to see manifested in one's perception.

The importance of inspiration and creativity

'When man solves the mystery of imagining, he will have discovered the secret of causation, and that is: imagining creates reality'.

Neville Goddard

It is the imagination and not the will which is the most important human faculty; and thus it is not one's will that one needs to train, but it is the training of the imagination that one has to develop. Unfortunately our society is set up to undermine people's imaginative unconscious and conscious capacity.

We are always foisted the doctrine of effort, where effort means will, and where will means forceful struggle in opposition with the effortless use of the imagination. **The will should just be used to hold the mind concentrated on a particular aim of effortless visualization and meditation.**

Always think that what you have to do is easy. In this state of mind you will not spend more of your strength than just what is necessary. If you consider it difficult, you will spend ten times more strength than you need and you will waste a lot of energy.

What is called creativeness or creativity is only the power of becoming aware of what already is in potentiality. The whole of creation is already finished. Creativity is only a deeper receptiveness of the entire contents of all time and all space while experienced in a time sequence, but which actually coexist in an infinite and timeless now.

How to work with intention and primary causation

The power to manifest a 'demonstration' depends entirely upon one's spiritual power and for this to succeed there are three steps: intention or idealization, visualization, and materialization.

One should therefore start by focusing the attention to a place where there are no causes or circumstances, the Expanse of Pure Being itself which is one's nature, and from there dictate what circumstances shall be through primary causation, and then leave the circumstances to take care of themselves without the interference of opposing beliefs.

Even better is to concentrate not on particularized circumstances of health, love and prosperity but on health, love and prosperity themselves, the attributes of Pure Being, the real nature of the individual.

Primary causation has unlimited creative power to start a new sequence of causation, and it is not bound by inevitable effects which would flow from past thoughts and actions. It is not habitual compulsive thinking which is always bound to prior causes and conditions. Through the methods of primary causation we work with the effect to establish the necessary primary causes for its manifestation as self-perceived reality.

By using the methods of primary causation we eliminate from our consciousness all consideration of conditions which imply limitations, we plant a seed which, if left undisturbed, will infallibly germinate into a perceived fruition, remembering always that there is usually a time gap between the cause and the eventual effect which always depends on other secondary conditions or circumstances to manifest.

To give an example, observe the sky on a sunny day and reflect on how it could be raining the following day, or the opposite on a rainy day how could one imagine the next day to be a sunny and clear day. **The answer lies in the fact that the primary causes for both rain and clear sky were already present although invisible to the senses.** And so in the same way we can set in motion primary causes now which will manifest later, even though from an outside viewer there are no signs of what is about to happen.

One must also remember that it is not oneself which contributes to the efficacy of this method, just like Christ said: *'It is not I that doeth the works, but the Father that dwelleth in me, He doeth the work'.* One should simply create the perfect ideal and comply with the Laws of Reality which will bring about the result.

Primary causation through creative imagination, positive statements or prayer, functions like a sort of magnet able to draw to oneself those conditions which correspond in kind to the created ideal in a *'likes attract likes'* fashion. *'Thoughts are things'* is the Hermetic axiom, and the ideal becomes manifest.

This creative power depends upon our recognition of the potential power of one's spiritual nature and must not be confused with evolution. Creation is the calling into existence of that which does not exist in the objective world but in ideation. Evolution, on the other hand, is simply the unfolding of potentialities involved in things which already exist in self-perceived reality.

It is good, however, to remember that while every effect is the result of a cause, the effect in turn becomes a cause, which creates other effects, which in turn create still other causes; so that when you put the law of causation into operation you must remember that you are starting a train of causation for good or bad which may have endless possibilities.

The effect will always depend upon the mental image from which it emanates; this will depend upon the depth of the impression, the predominance of the idea, the clarity of the vision and the boldness of the image.

Cornelius Agrippa, one of the greatest authors of Renaissance occult philosophy, gives in his *'De occulta philosophia'* many instances of the power of the imagination: 'our soul causes much through faith; a firm confidence, an intent vigilance, and a resolute devotion, lend strength to the work which we would accomplish. We must, therefore, for every work, for each application to any object, express a powerful desire, flex our imagination, and have the most confident trust and the firmest belief, for this contributes immensely to a success'.

Fabio Paolini borrowed this Agrippan notion and explained it in the following statement: 'Some people assert that the feelings and conceptions of our souls can, by the force of our imagination, be rendered volatile and corporeal, and will obey us in whatever we want'.

As we have seen, things which seem miraculous in reality have a perfectly natural cause or causes, if they seem extraordinary it is only because one doesn't know the causes behind them.

'Thou shall also decree a thing, and it shall be established unto thee: and the light shall shine upon your ways'.

Job 22:28

On how to deal creatively with life's circumstances

'For the pagans run after all these things, and your heavenly Father knows that you need them. But seek first his kingdom and his righteousness, and all these things will be given to you as well'.

Matthew 6:32/33

Even though all the skilful methods explained in this book are very useful and can be of great help, one must remember that **the ultimate and foremost way to deal with life's circumstances (and death) is to become aware of one's own true nature as a lucid Expanse of Pure Being beyond time and space, beyond confusion and concepts, beyond suffering and relative circumstances, and integrate in that knowledge one's existence**

as a pure experience of the illusory play of Reality, the illusory adornment of Pure Being.

On the more relative level, the two qualities that we have to develop more than any others are love and faith or confidence in one's spiritual nature. These are the marks of Awakening: a love that embraces all, and faith that holds on to the invisible and the spiritual, in spite of the sternest tests and trials of one's life.

Being love itself in all our thoughts and actions leads us to happiness and vitality. We love for the sake of loving, just as the sun shines upon all for the sake of giving out its energy and not in order to receive back something in exchange. But, although this is our motive, yet we cannot escape being blessed, for love is life and hate is death.

We may want to have an easy, uneventful life, full of peace and enjoyment, and do not desire any 'harsh experiences' but this is equivalent in wanting to enjoy heaven before becoming fit to enter such a state.

In this regards, we need to bear in mind that if we desire to experience something we just have to put the causes for that to happen, and if we don't want something to happen we have to eliminate the causes for the potential event to manifest. Then we need to develop patience and wait for the secondary causes to do the rest.

If worry follows we deny its existence and affirm perfect peace, perfect wisdom, perfect knowledge, perfect understanding.

Affirm that you are a perfect spiritual being, indivisible from God, and, therefore, in your true nature, you can never be perplexed or troubled by the trivial things of the material life.

Again and again the worry will come, but if we will each time deny it and affirm our perfect primordial nature, the possessor of all wisdom and knowledge and understanding, the thought will get weaker and weaker until it is dissipated altogether.

If, for example, you have a persistent worry, just as you are going to sleep, after observing the worry thought and rising superior to it in your perfect world of Pure Being, simply hold the problem in your mind in an expectant way, believing and affirming that in the morning the problem will be solved. When the morning arrives you will find on awaking, the solution of your perplexity or it will come to you as you are getting up and going through the day.

'Reality is merely an illusion, albeit a very persistent one'.

Albert Einstein

How to pray for a change of perception and conditions

'Do not be anxious about anything, but in every situation, by prayer and petition, with thanksgiving, present your requests to God. And the peace of God, which transcends all understanding, will guard your hearts and your minds in Christ Jesus'.

Philippians 4:6-7

The method of prayer is one of the most powerful and skilful method, especially when nothing else works.

In this case one must understand that God does not change the 'modus operandi' of the Universe in order to comply with one's requests, nor does it make exception form one being to another, but it does act through well defined laws, and these laws can be placed into operation, consciously or unconsciously, by accident or deliberately and especially by prayer.

It is the operation of these marvellous laws which have caused men in all ages and in all times to believe that there must be a personal being called God or beings (the gods and angels of heaven) who responded to their petitions and manipulated events in order to meet their demands.

Supplicating and begging things to God without a proper understanding doesn't bring any result, **it is the prayer which is**

the realization that all things are accomplished, even before the prayer is made, that receives the answer.

It is not a question of getting something, because all things are possessed already, it is the realization of the fact that we are already accomplished and whole which produces what we call answer to prayer.

The true meaning of prayer is therefore thanksgiving and acknowledgment that oneself is a perfect spiritual Pure Being and therefore perfect and accomplished as it is.

But, of course, since we all have identified with a narrow and separate ego-self from immemorial time and therefore have all our particular desires and fears, it is only natural to pray and ask for whatever our heart is longing for at that particular moment.

Faith too is the realization that our prayers are already answered through the operation of the thought forces in the form of an earnest desire, coupled with expectation to its fulfilment.

And in the degree that the earnest desire thus sent out is continually held to and watered by firm expectation and faith, in just that degree does it either draw to itself, or does it change from the unseen into the visible, from the spiritual into the material, that for which it is sent.

Let the element of doubt or fear enter in, and what would otherwise be a tremendous force will be so neutralized that it will fail of its realization.

In reality, when one employs the method of prayer in order to change one's circumstances and events, it is always oneself (one's nature of Pure Being) which becomes a catalyst for the all pervading power intrinsic to oneself (as Pure Being) to act in order to comply with one's requests.

We can name four important factors involved in the method of prayer:

- The first factor is that although whatever happens in our lives manifests according to unerring laws set in motion by ourselves, like the Law of Cause and Effect and the Law of Vibration, by praying earnestly and with faith and confidence in the result, we assume the mental attitude of confident expectation, which is one of the most important factor in attaining a desired effect. Proof of this is Christ statements:

'Whatsoever things you ask for when you pray, believe that you receive them, and you shall have them'. Mark 11:2.4

The present tense in this sentence wants us to have absolute confidence that our prayers will be answered to our best interest and that we should feel as if we had already received what we have asked for as a prerequisite for receiving it. There is nothing more important than faith or confidence in the expected result. In another statement Christ says:

'For to the one who has, more will be given, and he will have an abundance, but from the one who has not, even what he has will be taken away'. Matthew 13:12

Here Christ is hinting at the Law of Cause and Effect, in the sense that abundance is based on accumulated causes of merit and it will manifest only in such a case. The one who hasn't got the causes (merits) of abundance will lose (or consume) even the little one has already accumulated.

Another interpretation is that we are only able to express in physical reality what we are conscious of being at the level of inner reality of consciousness or mind. Only to the one who is already content and can appreciate what he/she already has, more will be given, but from the one who is complaining for the little he/she has, all will be taken away.

- The second important factor is that in asking earnestly through prayer, and expecting faithfully, we unconsciously develop the mental image in our mind of the conditions desired and therefore we are able to set in motion a primary cause which, through the Law of Cause and Effect and the Law of Vibration, will materialize our ideals. In fact faithful prayer is one of the most powerful forms for setting in motion primary causes.

- The third important factor is that **by praying to what we regard as a holy object we unconsciously develop the qualities associated with the concepts we have of that object.** For example if we pray to Christ, Buddha or God, with the belief that they are the embodiment of love, health, prosperity, wisdom and compassion, automatically, we develop these qualities, which as we have seen, are our natural and spontaneous qualities of Pure Being, and therefore we place ourselves in an harmonious position in regard to the attainment of more love, health, prosperity, wisdom, compassion and all our desires are fulfilled.

- The last very important factor is that all beings in the infinite Universes are not separate from one another but are *individually* integrated as 'the totality of Pure Beings's adornment'. **Therefore we can understand that on a subtle level we all affect one another according to the interdependence of causes and conditions,** and because of this, through prayer one can 'receive' help from higher beings or angels and archangels *interdependently* or in a way that doesn't contradict the primary causes that one has set in motion through the Law of Cause and Effect and the Law of Vibration.

An example would be that Christ, Buddha or gods would indeed 'help' us getting prosperity, health, love and better life conditions *interdependently* with the causes of generosity, empathy and love we have set in motion at least at the level of our mind (Law of Cause and Effect) and our confidence in the desired effect (Law of Vibration). **Of course it would be impossible to receive 'help' from another being if we were to set in motion causes in**

opposition to what we are asking for or if we placed ourselves in an opposite vibration to our fulfilled desires.

Moreover, since all those who have already realized themselves as indivisible from the State of Pure Being are beyond time and space and can take any form according to circumstances, prayers are already heard as soon as are uttered without the need for petition and begging.

Bearing in mind that, since the 'generic character' of Pure Being can be summed up in the words *'always goodness'* (beyond the relative concepts of good and evil), if we were to develop qualities contrary to its generic character, this inversion would place us in a position of powerlessness and frustration and our prayers would go unanswered.

On the principle of faith and confidence

'Faith is the substance of things hoped for, the evidence of things not seen'.

Hebrews 11:1

Gratitude should be given in advance, not after the fulfilled desire. This is because to **thank in advance for something is the highest form of faith**. It is a statement of supreme confidence and it is the ultimate knowing of the Truth.

One may ask how I can truthfully affirm that I am that which I know myself not to be. **The answer is that you are not relying on the finite and limited self-grasped personality, but on the great and glorious spiritual Pure Being which is the real you. The former is a weak and coarse reflection of the latter.** This glorious and real you is perfect and lives in a perfect spiritual world. When you affirm in your perfect spiritual world that you are perfect you mean the real and spiritual you, and you are telling the truth about yourself.

72

Whatever quality you then affirm is completely true, because the real you is primordially self-perfected. By denial of evil and imperfection and by the affirming of infinite self-perfection you dissolve evil in your life and bring it more into harmony with the perfect spiritual life. Therefore what you affirm in your perfect mental world, is later, and sometimes instantaneously, manifested in your self-perception of the material world.

The best way to pray for a change of circumstances is then to recognize yourself as that which you now desire through the realization of your nature of Pure Being.

In final analysis, it is the prayer which is the realization that all things are accomplished even before the prayer is made, that receives the answer quickly. It is not a question of getting something, because all things are possessed already as adornment of Pure Being, but it is the realization of this fact which produces what we call answer to prayer.

'But when you pray, go into your room, close the door and pray to your Father, who is unseen. Then your Father, who sees what is done in secret, will reward you'.

Matthew 6:6

On how to overcome the habit of worrying about relative circumstances

'Take delight in the Lord, and he will give you the desires of your heart'.

Psalm 37:4

One of the reasons for anxiety and depression is the feeling of "powerlessness' in relation to one's life circumstances and also one's own mind churning out nasty negative thoughts and emotions in response to them. Attachment to a sense of identity and the constant need of confirmation and security is also another reason for fear and worry. Unfortunately no one is immune to this and mind's training is the best solution as it brings a feeling of newly found power over one's mind, **but this is a training of a lifetime not a month or a year.**

'Can any one of you by worrying add a single hour to your life? And why do you worry about clothes? See how the flowers of the field grow. They do not labor or spin. Yet I tell you that not even Solomon in all his splendor was dressed like one of these. If that is how God clothes the grass of the field, which is here today and tomorrow is thrown into the fire, will he not much more clothe you—you of little faith'?

Matthew 6:27-30

Even though Christ clearly tells us to have faith, even when all our physical needs are met, and there is no immediate threat or danger, we seldom feel at ease. On the contrary we may spend hours worrying about situations that could occur, but almost never do.

Along with such feelings come an almost endless procession of thoughts of worries about how we could be more at peace, and yet ironically, a worried mind is, by definition, not at peace. This is the sad joke about human beings, that we are all so busy worrying whether or not we are going to be at peace in the future that we don't give ourselves the chance to be at peace in the present.

We must remain in the field of the present moment and embrace uncertainty and impermanence with the whole confidence that nothing can disturb our self-perfected nature of Pure Being, our real 'selfless self'.

Let's take a look at these statements from the Bible to help us find confidence and dissolve fear and worry:

'If you can'?' said Jesus. 'Everything is possible for one who believes.'

Mark 9:23

'Therefore I tell you, do not worry about your life, what you will eat or drink; or about your body, what you will wear. Is not life more than food and the body more than clothes? Look at the birds of the air; they do not sow or reap or store away in barns, and yet your heavenly Father feeds them. Are you not much more valuable than they'?

Matthew 6:25-26

'So do not worry, saying, "What shall we eat?" or "What shall we drink?" or "What shall we wear?" For the pagans run after all these things, and your heavenly Father knows that you need them. But seek first his kingdom and his righteousness, and all these things will be given to you as well. Therefore do not worry about tomorrow, for tomorrow will worry about itself. Each day has enough trouble of its own'.

Matthew 6:31- 34

'Truly I tell you, if anyone says to this mountain, "Go, throw yourself into the sea", and does not doubt in their heart but believes that what they say will happen, it will be done for them'.

Mark 11:23

'Very truly I tell you, whoever believes in me will do the works I have been doing, and they will do even greater things than these, because I am going to the Father'.

John 14:12

'What I feared has come upon me; what I dreaded has happened to me'.

Job 3:25

The point is that we are either worrying or we are praying and confidently expecting the blessings we desire because these two things do not go together. Detachment and confident expectation are the antidotes to worry. When you realize that you are that unchanging timeless and all pervading Awareness of Pure Being, how can you be afraid of people and circumstances?

When we are confronted with an unsolvable situation, we need to remember the following statements:

'For no word from God will ever fail'.

Luke 1:37

'If a problem is fixable, if a situation is such that you can do something about it, then there is no need to worry. If it's not fixable, then there is no help in worrying. There is no benefit in worrying whatsoever'.

The Dalai Lama

On judging others

'Why do you look at the speck of sawdust in your brother's eye and pay no attention to the plank in your own eye'?

Matthew 7:3

Never entertain an undesirable feeling of condemnation nor think negatively about any wrong in any shape or form in another person because to do so is to impress your own subconscious with these limitations. What you do not want done unto you, do not feel that it is done unto another.

The angry, condemning person, who sends out destructive thoughts, feelings, or speech to another, receives back to himself the qualities and feelings with which he charged this judging power; while the relaxed and positive person receives the energy which serves him to live a happy and balanced life. Thus, the creator of discord, through anger and condemnation, is unconsciously destroying himself, his world of activity, and his life as a whole.

'You hypocrite, first take the plank out of your own eye, and then you will see clearly to remove the speck from your brother's eye'.

Matthew 7:5

How to deal with negative thoughts and emotions

The Principle of Polarity and Rhythm states that contrasting and opposing feelings and emotions are in reality opposite poles of the same energy of Pure Being, and that the Principle of Rhythm is always in operation.

Knowing this, by shifting its polarity one may change a painful feeling or emotion into its opposite, distressing feelings may be changed in polarity, or balanced with their opposites.

One may change the polarity to its opposite to a sufficient degree in order to establish a balance and thus create a state of presence, which results in a peaceful state of mind. Since action and re-action are equal, one should always manage to have a push or a pull counteracted with a push or a pull in the opposite direction, and thus maintain a state of balance and presence.

One should never fight or struggle with an undesirable emotional quality by opposing a strong will to it, as this would be a waste of energy, and, worse more, it would reinforce that undesirable emotion.

Hate is not to be fought against with rejection and hate, since this only adds fuel to the fire of hate, instead one polarizes to its opposite of love to a degree as to find the right presence and balance.

One could also make use of creative imagination and positive statements, by first becoming aware of the negative emotion without rejecting it, and then create a visualized image as a symbol of its opposite and repeat a statement in one's mind until a state of peaceful presence is found.

In just the same way the emotional states of others may be influenced by polarizing their minds on the opposite pole of the scale of the emotion in question, for example by forming the mental image of love in one's own mind, and then concentrating its effects upon the other person.

There is always a point of balance between the poles of every pair of opposites, but that point exists only because the extremes exist, and in the central point is always found the power of the whole event. By abiding in peaceful presence one is able to use action and reaction without being subject to either.

One then is not enmeshed or conditioned by the emotional storms and one is able to handle the emotions as a master does an instrument, not giving oneself up to emotions as a passive slave or a blind tool, but always aware of the reaction and return of the emotional swing of rhythm.

A more advanced method would be to rise above polarity into the timeless peace of Pure Being which is one's real nature and let whatever thoughts and emotions dissolve by itself.

The training method that one can adopt, which we have already seen at the beginning of this chapter, consists in imagining yourself on a hot air balloon which is rising above the surface of the earth into the higher regions of the sky, rising above the lower planes of personality toward the higher planes of Pure Being.

As you rise, start throwing off the balloon all your likes and dislikes, loves and hates, preferences for and against anything and everything whatsoever either good or bad, in short the entire collection of inherited or acquired feelings, emotions and concepts which have formed the body of your ego-personality until now.

As the mental balloon rises higher and higher, allow yourself to be divested of even the more subtle feelings and emotions, concepts and ego identification, until finally you find yourself divested of every iota of personal character you ever possessed, and rest 'naked' in the always positive and blissful, timeless state of Pure Being, beyond any polarity.

In this way by rising above the swing of the plane of rhythmic emotions to the plane of Pure Being, one learns to value emotions and feelings for what they really are, pure energy adornments of one's real nature, and refuses to allow one's nature to become entangled in them.

In essence, whenever you become aware of negative thoughts and emotions arising, rather than ignoring them, rejecting them or fuelling them by obsessively trying to find a solution, identify, acknowledge, and remain present without judgment in their very presence and allow them to dissolve into the self aware Expense of Pure Being.

In a nutshell, one cannot keep evil or negative thoughts and emotions from coming, but one can certainly keep from entertaining them.

Positive affirmations and autosuggestions

'For by your words you will be acquitted, and by your words you will be condemned'.

Matthew 12:37

Words are the symbols of our thoughts and feelings, and a sentence is a combination of symbols.

The Principle of Vibration is expressed in statements and positive affirmations of the existence of the conditions which we wish to bring about. Just as the visualized mental images are the framework around which the actual material conditions form themselves, the statements, in the form of positive affirmations, are the pattern around which the visualized mental images form themselves. **The positive statement becomes that which is able to establish the primary causes for its manifestation.**

One should not say that such a condition will be, because that would affirm its lack in the present moment and give a negative suggestion to the timeless subconscious, but one should boldly assert the new conditions in actual being in the ever present timeless 'Now' of reality, affirming them earnestly and positively, in the present tense, avoiding all half-hearted statements, for they result in half-hearted results.

Statements should be employed preferably in a state of meditation and concentration and never publicly or loudly to other people. They are one's secrets.

If one wishes to connect and receive particular positive vibrations in the form of thoughts and feelings from others, one should develop a mental atmosphere or vibration corresponding with those vibrations one wishes to receive, and if one wishes to avoid vibrations of a certain kind, the best way is to rise above them in one's own mind, and to cultivate mental vibrations opposite to them.

One's direct experience and identification with the Expanse of Pure Being, one's nature, is the strongest and most positive 'state of vibration' one can produce or achieve.

'You will also declare a thing, And it will be established for you; So light will shine on your ways'.

Job 22:28

Examples of general positive affirmations

We constantly give ourselves subconscious autosuggestions, and usually not in our best interest, so now all we have to do is to give ourselves conscious positive autosuggestions, and the process consists in weighing carefully in one's mind the things which are to be the object of the autosuggestion, and repeat them several times believing fully and confidently in their meaning.

If the subconscious accepts this suggestion and integrates its meaning, the specific aim of the suggestion is realized in every particular.

These are just a few examples of positive statements, bearing in mind that you can invent or tailor these statements according to your needs or the type of capacities you would like to develop.

I am of the nature of Pure Being and Infinite Goodness (God).

I live, move, and experience everything as a self perception of Pure Being.

I am the nature of infinite love and compassion.

I am life, health and well being.

I am love and therefore I let love into my field of experience.

I let joy and fulfilment enter my field of experience.

All my desires are spontaneously fulfilled.

I am fulfilled and confident in all my activities.

Denials

Denials are an important part of working with autosuggestions when one is faced with stubborn and ingrained negative habitual tendencies or negative circumstances.

It is sometimes marvellous to see how the obstructing negative force disappears from one's mental world, which is followed by a response of the same kind and degree in the phenomenal world. Here are a few examples of denials:

I deny the illusion of all evil (poverty, illness, depression) out of my field of experience and self-perception.

I deny the illusion of disease and its causes out of my field of experience.

I deny fear and its causes out of my field of experience.

I deny the reality of any cause of fear.

I deny the illusion of doubt, frustration and loneliness out of my self-perception.

I deny that poverty is part of my essential nature.

I deny that anything or anybody can hurt my essential nature of Pure Being.

I deny the illusion of depression or powerlessness and their causes out of my field of experience.

I deny out of my field of experience all that is opposed to my state of well being.

'I deny the power of ... (such and such addiction) ...over my free will'.

I deny the power of such and such obstacle over me. I deny it out of my field of experience.

May the illusion of poverty, illness and frustration dissolve into the space-like Expanse of Pure Being.

Just as a branch withers and dies if the sap of the vine ceases to flow towards it, so do things in your phenomenal world pass away if you take your attention away from them.

To dissolve a problem that now seems so real to you all that you need to do is remove your attention from it in spite of its seeming reality, turn from it in consciousness and repeat a denial in your mind. Become indifferent and begin to feel yourself to be that which would be the solution of the problem.

How to manifest the self-perception of health, joy and fulfilment

'Have faith in God', Jesus answered. 'Truly I tell you, if anyone says to this mountain, "Go, throw yourself into the sea", and does not doubt in their heart but believes that what they say will happen, it will be done for them. Therefore I tell you, whatever you ask for in prayer, believe that you have received it, and it will be yours'.

Mark 11:22-24

Every time you think you send a message into the formless primordial energy field, which is none other than your timeless Awareness, from which and by which all things are manifested, this starts a train of causation which relates with the things that correspond with the image of your thought. If your thought is sufficiently refined and concentrated, then you will be placed in harmony with the object of your thought quickly, if not, more time will be required.

The universal laws of the Universe, work in a way that one will manifest into one's field of experience only those people, events and experiences that match one's state of being.

This is because we are only able to express in physical reality what we are conscious of being at the level of inner reality of consciousness or mind. If your circumstances are limiting and depressing, you can visualize how you'd like them to be in your mind and feel grateful that *'it will be done for you'*. **The most important fact to remember is that the signs of a 'demonstration' always follow and never precede your awareness of it.**

'For to the one who has, more will be given, and he will have an abundance, but from the one who has not, even what he has will be taken away'.

Matthew 13:12

When you can feel the joy of thanksgiving for having received that which is not yet apparent to the senses, you have definitely set in motion those primary causes which will manifest your desire.

An example of this is the story of Jesus feeding the crowds where he takes the seven loaves and the fish, and after he had given thanks, he breaks them and gives them to the disciples, and they in turn feed the people that had gathered in thousands.

You should therefore eliminate any possible tendency to complain of conditions as they have been or as they are now, because it rests within you to change them and make them what you would like them to be, by directing your effort to a realization of the spiritual resources always at your disposal, from which all real and lasting power comes.

You should persist in the practice of seeing things and feeling their reality in your imagination until you come to a realization of the fact that there can be no failure in the accomplishment of any proper aim in life if you understand your power and persist in your training, because the spiritual forces are always ready to lend themselves to a purposeful intention in the effort to crystallize thoughts and desires into actions, events, and conditions.

God's imagination, containing all that is needed, reproduces itself in the human imagination; therefore, all things exist in the human imagination. Everything is created by the human imagination as God's adornment. Therefore visualize yourself giving the very highest and best service of which you are capable of and then picture the highest good coming back to you in return.

To seek on the outside for that which you do not feel you are in consciousness is to seek in vain because we never find that which we want but only that which we most intimately are. As a consequence we can express and manifest only that which we are conscious of being: *'To him that has it is given'.*

If you change the concept of yourself, the events ahead of you in time are altered and will form again a deterministic sequence starting from the moment of this changed concept. You have the power of intervention, which enables you, by a change of consciousness, to alter the course of observed events.

Just like a tree doesn't withhold its nourishment from the leaf, neither does our true nature withhold abundance from us as in reality we are indivisible. In fact everything is our own self-perception and if we do not possess a life of ease and contentment is because we persist in negative thinking, complaining and because we don't claim to be that which we desire to be.

'As the Great Teacher said: "Don't you believe that I am in the Father, and that the Father is in me? The words I say to you I do not speak on my own authority. Rather, it is the Father, living in me, who is doing his work"'.

John 14:10

The principle of inverse transformation

The principle of inverse transformation states that if an effect (a) can be produced by a cause (b), then inversely, the same effect (a) can produce the cause (b).

For example, just like heat can produce mechanical motion, so can mechanical motion produce heat and if electricity can produce magnetism, magnetism too can develop electricity.

In just the same way, if a physical event can produce a specific feeling and a psychological state, a psychological state or feeling can manifest a physical event.

Therefore whatever you want to be or achieve can only be obtained by assuming the feeling of the desired state in your mind, since it is your mind which is the creator of your objective reality.

It is a misconception to think that, other than persistently assuming the feeling of the wish fulfilled, one can do anything to help the realization of the desire one wishes to obtain, because doing something means introducing the element of effort and obstacle.

Instead, an assumption, conscious or unconscious, will direct all thoughts and action spontaneously to their fulfilment following the path of the least effort.

The time it takes to achieve any aim is directly proportional to how natural it is for you to be what you want to be or have what you want to have. This feeling of naturalness can be easily achieved by persistently filling your mind with imagining yourself being what you want to be or having what you desire and you must fill yourself with this feeling until it is completely natural to you.

The essential requirement being that in your imagination and in your mind all things are possible and natural.

If the senses seem to suggest the opposite, deny the evidence of the senses, and continue to assume the feeling of the wish fulfilled until a feeling of naturalness is achieved.

Receiving love

Real love is selfless and free from fear as it pours out without demanding anything in return. Love is our nature of Pure Being in manifestation and the strongest magnetic force in the Universe. Pure, unselfish love draws to itself its own reflection and it does not need to seek or demand, its joy is in the joy of giving.

Jealousy and insecurity are love's worst enemies, because they force the imagination to run wild with fear, and invariably these fears objectify if they are not dissipated in one's timeless nature.

Since by law you can never receive what you have never given, by giving a perfect and unselfish love, demanding nothing in return, you will indeed receive a perfect love in return.

Thoughts are forces and each comes back laden with the effect that corresponds to its cause, therefore, if you want the entire world to love you, you must first love the entire world because in the degree that we love we will be loved.

Any time you exercise your imagination lovingly upon another you have planted the seed for receiving perfect love from another because our selfless nature is the nature of Pure Love.

On the obstacles to the 'demonstration'

'Truly I tell you, if you have faith as small as a mustard seed, you can say to this mountain, "Move from here to there," and it will move. Nothing will be impossible for you'.

Matthew 17:20

The fact that it does not feel natural to you to be what you imagine yourself to be or to realize your aim is the reason of your failure. Regardless of your desire, regardless of how faithfully and carefully you follow the methods described in this book, if you do not feel natural about what you want to be or achieve you will not be able to obtain it.

The essential feeling of naturalness can be achieved by persistently and effortlessly filling your mind with the imagination that you are what you desire to be or have.

Since in the mind all things are possible and since we always experience only the projections of our mind, if your assumptions are not fulfilled, it is because of the deeply ingrained tendency of mistrust in your subconscious mind. However, this can be overcome by denying the evidence of the senses and appropriating the feeling of the wish fulfilled.

The main reason we boycott our desires is because we constantly judge the physical appearances of reality and consider it real, forgetting that the all reality is a state of self-perception.

Growth is attained through an exchange of the old for the new, of the good for the better; it is a conditional or reciprocal action at the level of mind which makes it possible for us to receive only as we give.

You must prepare for the things you have asked for even when there isn't the slightest sign of it in sight, bearing in mind that sometimes just before a big achievement there is apparent failure and discouragement.

If you persuade yourself that you can do a certain thing, provided this thing is humanly possible, you will do it however difficult it may be. If on the contrary you imagine that you cannot do the simplest thing in the world it will be impossible for you to do it regardless of easy it may actually be.

But if you have worked with autosuggestions and if your subconscious has assimilated the idea that you have been presenting it, you will soon see it manifested as your objective reality. Bear in mind that autosuggestions must also be in agreement with the subconscious imagination, for example if you think: 'I will make such and such thing happen' and the subconscious says: 'I want it, but it might be too difficult', not only you will not obtain your desire, but even exactly the opposite may happen.

A life of ease becomes possible only when we get rid of our finite personality and lose it in the formless and timeless Awareness which is our real nature.

Always start by abiding upon your real nature as Pure Being, a timeless Awareness with infinite potentiality. It is only when you realize the infinite perfection of yourself as a Pure Being that the imagination becomes reality.

The one who is centred in one's timeless nature through total confidence in one's power can overcome every storm with the same calmness and serenity that he faces any other event, for he knows that all is an illusory manifestation of self-perception.

To conclude, we must persistently believe the truth of the injunction: *'Rest in the Lord, wait patiently for Him and He shall give thee thy heart's desire.'* All shall be given to him who is ready to accept it, but we may have to wait for it in patience and confidence.

There is but one source of power in the Universe and that power is you. The Power is infinite, but the lack of faith makes it unavailable.

The need to banish all fears

'Jesus said unto him, If thou canst believe, all things are possible to him that believeth'.

Mark 9:23

In ultimate analysis there is no one to defend with fear and no one to satisfy with hope. One should rest beyond hope and fear within the knowledge of one's nature of Pure Being.

On the relative level, fear exists in your life by your permission only, not because it is needful as a warning against an outside 'evil'. Fear is usually induced by unduly magnifying an actual danger, and most often by conjuring up fictitious dangers through excessive or obsessive thinking.

If you want to realize fearlessness you must leave behind all that is now your present problem or limitation, by taking your attention away from it. Turn your attention away completely from every problem and limitation which induces the fear that you now possess.

When you come into the realization of your oneness with God's infinite life and power, and open yourself that it may work through you, you will find that you have entered upon an entirely new phase of life, and that all fear inducing thoughts will be left behind.

We can classify fears in various ways; for example, there are many types of mental fears like timidity, lack of confidence, weakness, anticipated or imagined failure etc. There are fears of animals, inanimate objects, physical forces, human beings, apparitions and hallucinations, demons, deities etc. Also there is fear of events of the present, future, imaginary, possible, probable, contingent, **but ultimately all fears are based on the fear of death of the ego-personality.**

The habit of fear will not dissolve until the mind has acquired a fixed habit of courage. Whatever establishes that habit, will soon undermine and finally dissolve the power of every variety of fear.

Start by substituting in your mind the idea of self-preserving reason for any kind of fear as your perpetual guard and guide. **Make it a profound conviction of your deepest self that no real harm can come to that self because you have recognized your selfless nature of timeless Pure Being.**

Affirm in your mind that you are one with the Primordial Mind and therefore you can never be perplexed or troubled by the trivial things of the material life. Again and again the worry will come, but if you each time deny it and affirm your perfect spiritual nature, the possessor of all wisdom and knowledge and understanding, the fear based thoughts will get weaker and weaker until they will disappear altogether.

If you have a persistent problem that is causing continuous distress or anxiety, simply hold the problem in your mind expecting a solution, believing and affirming that in the morning the problem will be solved. When the morning arrives you will find on awaking the solution of your problem or it will come to you during the same day or in the course of days.

On death and how to die

This book wouldn't be complete without a short mention to the natural process of death and dying.

The first thing to understand is who or what dies. If you have discovered in yourself the nature of Pure Being and you abide in this knowledge than there is no real death, just a process of letting go of what is naturally impermanent and transient, your body, thoughts, emotions which form your ego grasping finite personality.

When we die the identification with what is impermanent dissolves but the possibility of recognizing and abiding in the timeless nature is always available even after the physical death. **Then whatever may happen just let it happen, all is just an apparition, an experience of impermanent forms, thoughts and feelings that have no real essence but which are like the movements of the clouds in the sky as the adornment of Pure Being.**

Just like the sky and the sun are always there regardless of the forming and passing clouds, our immutable timeless nature is unborn and undying regardless of the transient nature of body, psyche and grasped personalities.

'Only those who have dared to let go can dare to re-enter'.

Meister Eckhart

Chapter 5

The science of healing

'Beware of this fatal error in spiritual healing. You do not heal - the Spirit does'.

William Walker Atkinson

Healing through prayer

As we have seen the method of prayer is very effective in discovering one's nature of Pure Being, in fulfilling one's wishes but also as a form of healing for oneself and others.

A famous study conducted by Professor Leonard Leibovici and published in the British journal of Medicine (BJM) entitled: 'Effects of remote, retroactive intercessory prayer on outcomes in patients with bloodstream infection: randomized controlled trial' proved that prayers made 4 to 6 years after the event were able to modify the outcome for the group of people that prayers were made. In fact it was associated with a shorter stay in hospital and shorter duration of fever in those patients for which prayers were made.

This study proves that linear time is an illusion and that the future can influence the past in the same way as the past influences the future.

Since everything happens in the ever present 'Now-ness' of timeless Awareness which is none other than one's timeless nature, everything we do and say can influence any event in time and space.

Every prayer and every wish we make for ourselves and others with a pure and compassionate heart and mind has an effect regardless of time and space.

Self Healing

Before you start a self healing session, start by telling your mind what you expect it to do for you, insist upon it to take hold of the physical body and restore its vital energy.

Then lying flat on the floor or bed, completely relaxed, with hands resting lightly over the solar plexus and breathe rhythmically in a relaxed and effortless manner. When the rhythm is fully established each inhalation will draw in an increased supply of vital energy from the infinite supply of Pure Being, which will be taken up by the nervous system and stored in the solar plexus.

At each exhalation the vital energy is being distributed all over the body, to every organ, to every muscle and every cell from the top of your head to the soles of your feet, invigorating, strengthening and stimulating every part of your mind/body complex.

While doing this try to form a mental picture of the inrushing vital energy, coming in through the lungs and being taken up at once by the solar plexus, then with the exhaling, being sent to all parts of the system, down to the finger tips and down to the toes.

Another method for general self healing is lying in a relaxed way, breathe in and out rhythmically, and command that a good supply of vital energy may be inhaled during each inhalation.

With each exhalation, send the universal vital energy to the affected part with the purpose of stimulating it, varying this occasionally by exhaling with the mental command that the diseased condition may be forced to dissolve and disappear. You can use the hands by passing them down the body from the head to the affected part.

In using the hands in healing yourself or others always hold the mental image that the universal vital energy is flowing down the arm and through the finger tips into the body, thus reaching the affected part and healing it.

If you feel that your vital energy is low or you feel exhausted the best thing is to place the feet close and to lock the fingers of both hands above your head in any way that seems the most comfortable, then breathe rhythmically always in a relaxed manner a few times, and you will feel the effect of recharging.

Another form of self healing is through 'thought directed energy' to the affected parts of the body.

When properly applied this form of healing produces a quick and direct effect, and therefore it is one of the simplest and best form of general healing treatment.

This form of healing is based upon the fact that the organs, the systems and even the cells of the body have a 'mind' in them. This 'mind' of the cells, responds to a strong thought impression from the 'conscious mind', particularly when the thought is heavily charged with the vital energy.

The healing process is actualized by directing highly charged thoughts to the 'mind' of the affected part, and by addressing it positively, either by uttering the actual words or by speaking them mentally.

You could suggest to the 'mind' of the part to be healed and you will be surprised at how readily the cells and organs will respond.

In a nutshell, you must never affirm an illness into your mind and life but only a temporary lack of health, and the same holds true for wealth, freedom, and fulfilment. By doing this you will begin to manifest better health and strength in your life.

Healing at distance

There is no better way to help others than to bring them to the knowledge of themselves and there is no better way to bring them to the knowledge of themselves than to lead them to the knowledge of their nature of Pure Being.

On a more relative level, if you want to become a healing channel for the inflow of the universal healing energy, you should fix the mind on the thought that you are now a 'spiritual channel' through which healing energy flows, and continue to mentally see or feel the inflow and outpouring of vital energy during the entire treatment.

You must always remember that no matter what the difficulty is, no matter where it is, no matter who is affected, you have no patient but yourself; you have nothing to do but to convince yourself of the truth which you desire to see manifested.

Since nearly all forms of healing create a new mental atmosphere and conditions in the patient, the first thing to do is to replace fear with confidence and the physical results will follow.

See the person you want to heal in your 'mind's eye' as you wish them to be. Then by clear visualization the transmission of healing energy is accomplished by a mere act of desire or will, in other words, by thinking of it as occurring in that moment.

Directing intention toward a distant person is correlated with activation of that person's autonomic nervous system. Strong motivation to heal and training on how to cultivate and direct compassionate intention may further enhance this effect.

On a practical level to treat people at a distance, you must form a mental image of them until you can feel yourself to be in close relationship with them. You can feel the sense of relationship when it is established as it will manifest a sense of closeness.

When the relationship is established, you mentally say to the distant patient, the following words: '*I am sending you a supply of vital energy, which will heal you*'. Then you can imagine the vital force as leaving your mind with each exhalation of rhythmic breathing, and travelling across 'spaceless and timeless intelligent space' instantaneously and reaching the person to be healed. This energetic healing stream directed by the thought of the sender may be projected to any person at a distance, as long as they are willing to receive it.

In giving mental healing treatments, the mind of the healer must be able to picture the desired conditions in the patient, which means to mentally see the patient as healed, and the systemic parts, organs and cells functioning normally.

In short, in the degree that the healer is able to mentally visualize the healing energy flow and the patient willing to receive it so will be the degree of success in mental healing. Try to dismiss all doubt from your mind, and train your mind to see the desired condition just as if it were actually before you in actuality.

Once the mental image, just described is formed, the thought is easily transmitted by merely thinking of it as occurring.

How to develop a protective aura

The aura is an egg shaped projection of fine particles of 'psychoplasm' representing one's 'personal protective field' and it is considered as the energetic frequency of the sum of all of one's thoughts, intentions and emotions. **As a form of an energy field it functions as a protective magnet, repelling or attracting vitality.**

The aura produces a 'mental atmosphere' which constantly surrounds oneself and makes oneself felt by those around.

Some beings radiate a feeling of positive energy through their aura, while others manifest just the opposite. Many likes and dislikes between people meeting for the first time, arise in this way, each finding in the mental atmosphere of the other, some harmonious or inharmonious element. **The character of the sum of one's thoughts and emotions may manifest as an aura of certain colours, which are visible to those having the capacity to perceive it.**

There is nothing so wonderful about this, when it is considered that the various 'colours' of light comprising the visible colours of the spectrum, ranging from red, on through orange, yellow, green, blue, indigo, and violet, arise simply from different rates of vibration.

The various colours may represent a particular emotion, for example the colour black represents hatred and malice, and gray represents selfishness and fear and so on.

One can employ simple visualizations in order to strengthen one's personal protective energy, bearing in mind that **the best method of protection is always to maintain a state of undistracted presence and an atmosphere of positive will and virtuous intention** which will strengthen one's personal power and make the vibration of one's being function as a shield against any adverse influences and circumstances.

A person whose mind is filled with love, courage and confidence may neutralize a multitude whose minds are filled with hate and evil due to the higher vibration of the positive pole. **The knowledge of one's ability to consciously radiate health, strength, and harmony will bring one into a realization of fearlessness.**

The creative visualization for personal protection:

In order to strengthen one's 'personal protective energy' one can employ this simple visualization: start by visualizing yourself as surrounded by a distance of about a meter with an egg-shaped field of highly charged positive atmosphere, radiating and vibrating with an intense energy. The important thing is to feel the immediate vicinity becoming charged with 'positive will power'. This type of phenomena is really existent, although the senses cannot perceive it.

If you feel under some sort of negative mental influence, you can mentally form a picture of your aura charged with an intense dark red will power similar to a firebrand, flowing outward repelling any adverse mental suggestions that are being sent to you and causing them to fly back to their source.

Alchemy and Spagyric medicine

Spagyria or spagyric medicine from the Greek 'spáein' to separate or extract and 'ágeirein' to combine, is a term first coined by the great physician and alchemist Paracelsus (1493 -1541).

According to Paracelsus the true purpose of Alchemy is not gold making, but rather the production of medicines to cure one's body and transform one's spirit. Paracelsus formulated that nature in itself was 'raw and unfinished' and man had the task to evolve things to a higher level using the spagyric method of separating and combining.

Spagyria maintains that a normal herbal extract could not be expected to contain all the medicinal properties from the living plant, and so the mineral component (ash) which is the result of the 'calcination' process, is prepared separately and then added back to potentiate the alcoholic herbal tincture.

The spagyric process separates and then recombines the three cardinal principles of Alchemy, which are Mercury, Sulphur and Salt to a 'heightened 'or 'alchemically potentiated' form.

- **Mercury:** The water element and the principle of fusibility (ability to melt and flow) and volatility, the alcohol extract of the plant carrying the plant's life essence. It represents the 'mind' of the plant.
- **Sulphur:** The fire element, the principle of inflammability, and the virtue of the plant, carrying the volatile oil essence of the plant. It represents the 'energy' of the plant.
- **Salt:** The earth element, the principle of fixity (non-action), representing the vegetable salts extracted from the 'calcinated' ashes of the plant. It represents the 'body' of the plant.

The herbal tinctures thus prepared have superior medicinal properties than a simple alcohol based herbal tincture, due to the formation of soap-like compounds from the essential oils and the basic salts contained within the 'calcinated' ash.

These spagyric compounds also include material from fermentation of the plant and also many aromatic components which are obtained through distillation.

Moreover, the alcohol used in true spagyric tinctures is not ordinary alcohol but 'spagyric alcohol', as one tries to eliminate all impurities contained in it.

The plant should then stand soaking in this hydro-alcoholic solution, which can vary from 45 to the 55 alcoholic volumetric degrees, for 30 days following the lunar cycle with a relationship of one kilo of plant dry residue to four litres of hydro-alcoholic solution (1/5).

The final spagyric herbal tincture is a powerful re-blending of all extracts into one 'healing essence' and can be used as a support to any healing treatment.

The Power intrinsic to Pure Being, our true nature, is always, ready and willing to be used by those who demand and use it, irrespective of the particular beliefs and theories or creeds of those using it.

Chapter 6

Concluding advice

'He that hath a bountiful eye shall be blessed, for he giveth of his bread to the poor'.

Proverbs 22:9

If you keep on patiently working in the unseen world of mind day after day you are bound to get results in due time.

When you have 'demonstrated' to yourself what you have learned in this book and brought harmony into your life and to those around you, do not get weary and neglect your daily work in the unseen world, because if you do so you will assuredly slip back to the old habits of negative patterns.

Since everything in your field of experience depends upon what you do in the unseen world of mind, do not forget to recognize daily your real nature of Pure Being, your oneness with God and all living beings, and renew your spiritual life which is the source of all your joy, fulfilment, success, accomplishment and health.

By working thus daily in the unseen world of mind of Pure Being you shall be in perfect harmony with yourself and others.

In ultimate analysis, until you don't realize your true nature of Pure Being and let that inner feeling become your primary state of being, frustration and strife will always seem real in your life.

The one who lives in the realization of the nature of Pure Being becomes a magnet to manifest as self-perception a continual supply of whatsoever things he desires for the benefit of all.

God has done already all the work that needed to be done, it only needs you to reveal its nature as a self-awareness. **Just like the natural flavour of sugar is sweet, the natural flavour of Enlightenment, Awakening as the nature of Pure Being, is love, wisdom and compassion.**

By vibrating thus in unison, aware of our true nature, through the powers and merits intrinsic to this divine nature, we are not only benefiting ourselves but we are also making the world a better world, and humanity a better humanity.

'Look inside of you, Sagredo, listen to your internal voice and remember that the true Teacher is Pure Being which whispers inside of yourself. Please listen to it: it is the Truth which is in you. You are divine, never forget this! We are not separating Sagredo, separation does not exist, we are all one in eternal contact with the Unique Soul'.

Giordano Bruno last testament before being burnt alive by the inquisition - February 1600

May the illusion of poverty, illness, frustration and death dissolve into the space-like non-dual nature of Pure Being.

Purum Esse Sustantia Omnium Rerum Est

Om Mani Padme Hum

Finis

About the Author

Max Corradi is a Life Coach, a Naturopathy practitioner and a musician. Since 1996 he has been studying and practicing the eastern and western traditions of inner knowledge, philosophy, Buddhist meditation, naturopathy and Self-Healing and he has been a student of many Tibetan Buddhist Teachers. He is also the author of complementary medicine and Self-Help books.

To contact the author please write to:

noageontology@gmail.com

Social media:

You tube: https://www.youtube.com/@noageontology1571/videos

Facebook:
https://www.facebook.com/groups/noageontology

Other books by the author

The seven Laws of Reality and Being
A manual about the Seven Hermetic Principles which govern
reality and phenomena Jaborandi Publishing

Low dose medicine
Healing without side effects using low dose cytokines,
interleukins, hormones, and neurotrophines
Jaborandi Publishing

Cures without side effects
Practical healing manual of the most essential and effective
biotherapy treatments
Jaborandi Publishing

No Age Ontology
The Joy of Timelessness
Jaborandi Publishing

Jaborandi Publishing 2023

jaborandipub@gmail.com

www.ingramcontent.com/pod-product-compliance
Lightning Source LLC
Chambersburg PA
CBHW052137090426
42741CB00009B/2124